From "Woe is Me" to "Wow is HE!"

Breaking Seven Core Curses
Invoking Seven Key Blessings

Dr. Douglas E. Carr

From "Woe is Me" to "Wow is HE!"

Breaking Seven Core Curses
Invoking Seven Key Blessings

Except where noted, the Scripture comes from the:

📖　New King James Version®. Copyright © 1982 by Thomas Nelson. Used by permission. All rights reserved.

Other Bible Translations used include:

📖 Amplified Bible (AMP) Copyright © 2015 by The Lockman Foundation, La Habra, CA 90631. All rights reserved.
📖 American Standard Version (ASV)Public Domain
📖 DARBY Public Domain
📖 King James Version (KJV) by Public Domain
📖 New American Standard Bible (NASB) Copyright © 1960, 1962, 1963, 1968, 1971, 1972, 1973, 1975, 1977, 1995 by The Lockman Foundation
📖 New International Version (NIV) Holy Bible, New International Version®, NIV® Copyright ©1973, 1978, 1984, 2011 by Biblica, Inc.® Used by permission. All rights reserved worldwide.

ISBN:1533553432
ISBN-13:9781533553430

DEDICATION

I dedicate this book first to all people everywhere who simply are done with low living and ready to advance the Kingdom of God, first within themselves, and then beyond themselves. May God increase His army who will apply the work of Calvary to break every curse and then step into every blessing God wants His children to enjoy through the completed work of Jesus' death, burial, resurrection, and ascension into heaven.

May we become like Jesus!

I also dedicate this book to Pamela Carr who is my best friend, wife, and partner in life and ministry. Only the Holy Spirit has taught me more about living a life of love, grace, continuing victory and sacrificial living than she. Pam remains my favorite hero and inspiration.

ACKNOWLEDGMENTS

I am grateful for the people of His House Foursquare Church, where I first preached this concept. I am also thankful for The Forgotten Man Ministry chaplains and inmates at the Branch County Jail where I tested this material to see if applied to people from all walks of life and levels of Christian experience.

I am always honored and grateful to have my wife and best friend, Pamela Carr, at my side. We had a type of "Burning Bush" experience while at the Releasing the Glory Conference at Shekinah Regional Kingdom Center in April this year (2016). We had been seeking how she might release me even more from the duties of "Lead Pastor" for His House Foursquare Church, because of my "now" call to expand the work of Doug Carr Freedom Ministries. When Apostle Barbara Yoder gave a call for "Senior Pastors" to come forward, I encouraged Pam to go and I remained in my seat – sensing I needed to stay out of the way until God did something special. When Apostle Barbara touched Pam, she went down in the Spirit and stayed down for an extended time. I went up and prayed over her until she tried to get up and immediately fell back down under the glory. She did this several times and I believe God elevated her even further in the ministry. May God richly bless her and help her bring the vision of true revival to our church and region.

Suzanne LeBlanc has been a wonderful help in countless ways. She proofread this book repeatedly and helped me work through countless computer issues with it. Thank you Suzanne!

My friends from the Sturgis Writer's Mill provided helpful insight on each chapter of this book.

ENDORSEMENTS

It is my privilege to meet with Dr. Douglas Carr and some other Kingdom pastors each month to pray for our community and the Kingdom work in our churches. This wonderful experience has given me insight into this man's heart for God and people. As pastors, we are well aware of the brokenness of people whom we have the opportunity to minister. We have seen how Jesus has made lives new that were broken. It was Jesus who said, "behold I make all things new." Through the power and the work of the Holy Spirit, the "woes" in this life are changed to "wows" for the glory of God. This is no small thing, my friend.

Over the years, Doug has helped countless people come to know the freedom that only comes through Jesus. He has helped them learn to walk and live in their new freedom by understanding that once set free from Satan's hold they are to live in the power of the Holy Spirit.

Doug's latest book, "From Woe is Me to Wow is HE" will be a blessing to all who read and apply the truth within its pages. Chapter eleven, "Praying It All the Way Through" is powerful, as is Chapter seven where Doug compares human hands being used for blessings or curses. *"From Woe is Me to Wow is He"* is a book showing the way from a broken and captive life to a life which has been set free, all for the glory of God. When the title of this book is lived out, people will be in awe of God and truly be blessed!

Rev. Bob L Renner
Sturgis Missionary Church
Sturgis, Michigan

Doug's latest book is a must read for every believer. He lays out the victory we can experience in seven key areas. He also points out our failure to experience the fullness of what God made available for us. Our ignorance of Satan and his machinations cause us to live below what God intended for us, often far below.

The ultimate key is a revelation of the power of the blood of Jesus. Doug lays out brilliantly and thoroughly why we fail to lay hold of this revelation. Satan has purposely set about to keep us in ignorance. We need to get back to basics, one being the power of the blood of Jesus.

This book will lead you into a whole new level of freedom and walking in the fullness of what God has for us. Once I started reading this, I couldn't stop. What a book! A must read by someone learning to walk in this fullness successfully.

Barbara J Yoder
Lead Apostle, Shekinah
Regional Apostolic Center
www.shekinahchurch.org
www.barbarayoderblog.com

CONTENTS

Breaking 7 Core Curses ~ Invoking 7 Key Blessings

FOREWORD BY BILL SUDDUTH

I have been ministering and teaching deliverance since my introduction to it during the Brownsville Revival in Pensacola, Florida; where I was a member of the pastoral care staff and head of the deliverance ministry. Doing deliverance is easy, but teaching people to address root causes so they can enjoy abundant blessing can be very difficult.

Dr. Douglas Carr's tenth and newest book, *"From Woe is Me to Wow is He!"* will prove helpful for deliverance ministers and everyone who is working out their own salvation with fear and trembling. Far too many people suffer ongoing effects of curses, either because they do not realize curses are a force to be addressed, or because they think every curse is broken and every blessing is released at the point of salvation. Being born again is the entrance to the Kingdom of God. Unfortunately, many converts stay in the foyer of the Kingdom rather than forcibly advancing fully into Kingdom life and power. Breaking curses, invoking blessings, and deliverance were a huge part of Christian growth and discipleship in the early Church and still must be.

In his introduction Doug addresses the devil's great lie that "Believers are automatically exempt from curses," by explaining how every generation since Adam and Eve has reinforced ancient curses. From there he explains how we can move from *"Woe is Me to Wow is He!"* He teaches how we can and should break seven core curses brought on the human race by man's repetition and reinforcement of original sin.

Doug carefully explains seven core curses, and how Jesus shed His precious blood in seven specific places, not only to break each of these curses but also to release seven key blessings! He includes specific prayers, to be used by individuals or groups, to break each of these curses and invoke each blessing.

I highly recommend this new resource by Dr. Douglas Carr, an active member of the International Society of Deliverance Ministers since its inception.

From Woe is Me to Wow is He! is a valuable new tool which will help many extend and secure the hard-fought for freedom of not only obtaining, but maintaining their victory over the schemes of the enemy.

Bill Sudduth
President, Righteous Acts Ministries, Inc.
Apostolic leader, International Society of Deliverance Ministers.
P.O. Box 64062, Colorado Springs, CO. 80962
Phone: (850) 390-4104
E-mail: office@ramministry.org
Website: www.ramministry.org

INTRODUCTION

Why do some Christians enjoy prosperous living and good health while others struggle continually with mental, emotional, physical, social, financial, and spiritual problems?

Is it because some people love Jesus more than others? Experience proves otherwise. Some Christians love Jesus with all their heart, soul, mind and strength, yet struggle more with problems and circumstances, seemingly beyond their control, than others who barely give Jesus a second thought.

Do some escape ongoing frustrations and problems because they are better equipped and educated in the things of the Lord? That doesn't seem to be the case. While education and discipleship are wonderful, some of the best trained and educated Believers suffer as much or more than others who have little training or discipleship.

Is it the devil's fault who comes to kill, steal, and destroy? Yes, but didn't Jesus come to give us abundant life? Absence of abundance in the lives of people who love Jesus, indicates they need to apply what Jesus did to their own lives and intentionally break seven specific curses and invoke seven specific blessings.

Kathi Moore, of the Sturgis Writer's Mill made this comment. "Our unconscious mind is much stronger than our conscious mind. If the unconscious mind has adopted a belief of, for instance, 'I don't deserve to be financially secure, or loved, or successful' then even if my conscious mind believes the Lord wants me to have abundant life, my subconscious mind will sabotage it."

I think Kathi has a good point which underscores the need to be transformed by the renewing of our minds so we can be aligned with the Word of God rather than the thoughts of our subconscious minds.

We can and should break every curse, engage in every blessing, and come into agreement with God's truth that Jesus came to give us abundant lives.

This does not imply Kingdom people won't face difficulties. Paul said trials and tribulations are part of the Kingdom journey.

📖 Strengthening the souls of the disciples, exhorting them to continue in the faith, and saying, "We must through many tribulations enter the kingdom of God." Acts 14:22.

Although we may face tribulations as we advance in the Kingdom of God, Jesus calls us to break every curse and invoke every blessing He purchased for us through His blood.

In the Old Testament, there are lists of curses which come upon the disobedient and their descendants. There are lists of blessings too, for the obedient and their children. In the New Testament Jesus said "If you love me, you will obey me." Loving obedience, however, does not make people exempt from curses until they *intentionally* break them through the blood of Jesus.

In one of my wife's messages, Pamela mentioned the Old Testament, the New Testament, and the "Now Testament." She understands the Bible has thirty-nine Old and twenty-seven New Testament books. She recognizes, however, God is still speaking and bringing us into greater revelation of what is already written in the Word. She calls this new understanding of the Bible the "Now Testament." Thank God for all the new books written on the principles of God's Word. Holy Spirit continues to inspire new books which are not part of the Canon of Scripture, any more than Bible Commentaries are, even when they are inspired.

God has, however, inspired authors to write on deliverance, healing, the Kingdom, and the like. Hopefully their books explain what God is doing *now* as He brings His people into greater understanding of what Jesus did, and what He wants Kingdom people to do. I hope He even will do so through my writing about Jesus' blood and its power to break curses and release blessings.

People need to individually apply what Jesus did for the whole world, in order to enjoy His blessings personally. Jesus died on the cross for every person. God is not willing for any to perish. John the Baptist introduced Jesus saying "Behold the Lamb of God who came to take away the sin of the world." Our Heavenly Father loves us so much He gave His only begotten Son that *whosoever* believes in Him will not perish but have everlasting life.

Jesus took our sins upon Himself so we might receive Him, believe on His name and be born again. Since God so loved the world, and since "He who knew no sin became sin so we might be made righteous," then why are so many still lost and hell bound? Either they have not heard the good news, or they have heard it but have not personally applied what Jesus did to their own lives, and therefore have not engaged in the fullness of His redemption.

Jesus came to destroy the works of the devil, but James tells us to resist the devil and he will flee. If we do not resist, the devil does not flee, even though Jesus came to destroy the devil's works. We have to *apply* what Jesus did through resisting, in order to enjoy the benefit of His work of deliverance.

One of the most frustrating things we face when witnessing is people who think they can be saved without believing in Jesus and personally receiving Him as Savior and Lord. A great frustration of deliverance ministers is people thinking they can be delivered from demons without resisting them. It just isn't so!

The same is true in breaking curses. It is disheartening to see people living under an obvious curse and watch them give into the curse because they can quote how Jesus became a curse *for* us (Galatians 3:13). Yes, He did, but we need to *apply* what He did to enjoy it personally!

If a person does not engage with Jesus' sacrifice for his or her salvation, by believing in and receiving Christ, that person remains lost, in spite of what Jesus did for him or her. If a person doesn't engage with Jesus by resisting demons, the demons remain even though Jesus gave us authority to cast them out. If a Christian does not apply what Jesus did to break curses and release blessings, that person remains under those curses and fails to enjoy the blessings God offers them.

Abiding in Jesus includes partnering with Him to work out our salvation with fear and trembling. We are not pawns, moved here and there by God's hand. Jesus calls us to take His yoke and partner with Him. We are to forcibly advance the Kingdom, beginning in our own lives.

We partner with Jesus to inherit salvation. We partner with Him to be set free from demons. We also need to partner with Jesus to break seven specific curses and inherit seven specific blessings. Jesus shed His blood in seven specific places to break seven specific curses and release corresponding blessings.

How I wish someone had taught me this when I began my Christian walk. I never even thought about the specific places Jesus shed His blood until I read the book *"The 7 Places Jesus Shed His Blood"* by Larry Huch.[1]

God changed my life through what I read in Larry's book years ago. The truths about Jesus breaking seven curses by shedding His blood in seven places has become part of me. I continually apply the blood of Jesus to break curses, release God's blessings, and cast out demons assigned to keep people under specific curses. The seeds of what God planted in me through Larry Huch have germinated, grown, and are producing fruit for the Kingdom.

Since Larry introduced me to this subject I have studied it in the Bible and have read countless articles and sermons others have written on the seven places Jesus shed His blood. How I wish I could have discovered this before I went through the most woeful time in my own life.

My ignorance of the need to apply Jesus' work in breaking curses nearly destroyed me after 15 years of Christian living and 14 years of ministry. Even though I read through the Bible every year, I missed out on so much Jesus did for me simply because I lacked knowledge how to apply what I read. Hosea warns us of this danger.

📖 My people are destroyed for lack of knowledge. Because you have rejected knowledge, I also will reject you from being priest for Me; Because you have forgotten the law of your God, I also will forget your children. Hosea 4:6.

Lack of knowledge about Jesus' blood exposes us to curses we do not have to put up! Jesus' blood is more powerful than we can ever imagine. It goes beyond salvation, healing and deliverance. Jesus' blood was also shed to break every curse. The word "saved" in the New Testament comes from the Greek word "sozo" which means "to make completely whole."

Jesus' blood was shed so we can be born again, regenerated, healed, delivered, prosperous, and set free to walk in His authority and power! He came to destroy the devil's work, "If the son sets you free, you will be free indeed."

We claim we are more than conquers through Christ who loved us. So why do people of faith continue to struggle with their health, attitudes, finances, emotions, addictions, relationships and the like?

Could it be that we lack the knowledge of Jesus' blood which was shed in seven places to specifically break the power of every curse over our lives? Have we or have we not overcome the devil by the blood of the lamb and the word of our testimony? We can win every personal battle through the blood of Jesus.

Barbara Yoder says we need to get back to the basics, including the blood of Jesus and its power to set captives free. Peter shares about the power of Jesus to deliver us from aimlessness.

📖 Knowing that you were not redeemed with corruptible things, like silver or gold, from your aimless conduct received by tradition from your fathers, but *with the precious blood of Christ*, as of a lamb without blemish and without spot. 1 Peter 1:18-19 (Italicized for emphasis).

The blood of Jesus was shed in seven places so we can resist the devil and make him flee. Jesus did His part. The same is true with breaking curses. Now we must apply His blood individually to break personal and ancestral curses and resist the devil.

I pray the Lord's Prayer nearly every day. I camp out on each phrase. For example, when I pray "our," I pray for my wife, myself, our five children, 24 grandchildren, and 3 great grandchildren, and for the people in our church. When I pray "Father" I come against orphan spirits, rejection, and abandonment and pray release of the Spirit of Adoption so each one will call out "Abba, Father." Jesus taught us how to pray and we can identify seven places of power in the Lord's Prayer, which are: Relationship, Praise, Kingdom, Will, Provision, Forgiveness, and Deliverance from temptation and the evil one.

There were seven places of power and anointing in the Old Testament tabernacle, which housed the presence of God. Now we are the tabernacle of God. We have the presence of God with a new covenant -- the sevenfold blood covenant. In Leviticus 16, people brought two goats to the tabernacle. One goat was for the atonement of sin. The second goat was to have the blood of the first goat placed on its head and then be released into the desert. Notice the word seven again:

📖 He is to take some of the bull's blood and with his finger sprinkle it on the front of the atonement cover; then he shall sprinkle some of it with his finger *seven times* before the atonement cover. He shall sprinkle some of the blood on it with his finger *seven times* to cleanse it and to consecrate it from the uncleanness of the Israelites. Lev. 16:14, 19 NIV (Italicized for emphasis).

Jesus' blood was shed seven times in seven different places! As we come to understand His blood was shed seven times, and in seven places with seven specific intents, we will learn to apply His blood to every area of curse and iniquity so we will know true "sozo" -- complete wholeness in and through the blood! We will look at the first of those curses and blessings after we consider the phrase "no curse without a cause."

Before we move into that, let me explain the sub-title *"Breaking Seven Core Curses ~ Invoking Seven Key Blessings."*

Curses always have a cause, often going as far back as Adam and Eve. In any case, whether the cause of a curse is personal or inherited, the curse is there until it is *deliberately* broken.

I wanted to use "engaging" in the sub-title, because we need to be intentional about going after the blessings Abba Father has for us in Christ Jesus. During one Daily Listening Room (where I sit and intentionally listen to the Lord and record what He says) however, the Lord changed the word from "engaging" to "invoking." I didn't understand at first, and "invoking" sounded religious to me, but I looked it up and now understand why God wants us to break curses and *invoke* blessings.

Consider the definition of invoke:
1. Invoke, verb (used with object), invoked, invoking.
2. to call for with earnest desire; make supplication or pray for:
3. to invoke God's mercy.
4. to call on (a deity, Muse, etc.), as in prayer or supplication.
5. to declare to be binding or in effect: to invoke the law; to invoke a veto.
6. to appeal to, as for confirmation.
7. to petition or call on for help or aid.
8. to call forth or upon (a spirit) by incantation.
9. to cause, call forth, or bring about.[2]

As we consider curses and blessings it helps to understand how the first Adam, of "Adam and Eve" fame, brought curses upon humans which affect personal and ancestral health, character, prosperity, productivity, dominion, and fragmentation. In the next chapter we will discuss how those curses have been reinforced from generation to generation.

The second Adam, Jesus Christ, redeemed for mankind the possibility for Christians to move back into blessing. We can "work out our salvation with fear and trembling" (Philippians 2:2) by applying what Jesus did when He shed His blood in seven specific places. Greater freedom and blessing will come to those who intentionally break each of the seven core curses and invoke each of the seven key blessings, which is the main focus of this book. First however, we will look at the cause behind curses.

Endnotes Introduction:

[1]Huch, Larry, *The 7 Places Jesus Shed His Blood.* Whitaker House, 2000, 2004.
[2]Source unknown from one of my old messages.

Scriptures referred to but not quoted chapter and verse in this chapter include: John 10:10; Deuteronomy 28:1-68; John 14:15, 23; 2 Peter 3:9; John 1:29, 3:16, 1:12; 2 Corinthians 5:21; 1 John 3:8; Galatians 3:13; James 4:7-8; John 15:4-6; Philippians 2:12; John 8:36; Romans 8:37; Revelation 12:10-11; John 1:14; Matthew 6:9-15; Luke 11:2-4.

CURSE WITHOUT A CAUSE?

Many lack understanding of how Believers can be affected by a curse. They quote verses like:

📖 Like a flitting sparrow, like a flying swallow, So *a curse without cause shall not alight.* Proverbs 26:2 (Italicized for emphases).

The error of thinking "there is no cause for a curse because of personal holiness" is such thinking is too individualistic. People think "the cause" is totally personal. If they have received Christ and taken care of personal "curse-causers" they think they are exempt from any curse. Their life experience, however, often proves otherwise. Let me illustrate, I live in Sturgis, Michigan, and actually lived on US 12 for over sixteen years. US 12 began as a trail Native Americans traveled from Detroit to Chicago and back. Over time the trail became packed down and grew wider. It was called "The Saulk Trail."

Then migration began from the East to the Midwest. Settlers packed the trail down further with their horses and wagons. In the early twentieth century automobiles widened the path and deepened its footprint. Soon gravel was added and logs were laid over soft and swampy areas and covered with gravel, making what was called "corduroy roads."

The name of the trail, now a major road, changed from The Saulk Trail to Chicago Road, then to US 112, and now is US 12. Semi-trucks and trailers soon began rushing between Detroit to Chicago with heavy loads. Pavement was added, lanes widened, and US 12 was packed down with the footprint of several generations.

Each generation added to the iniquitous footprint of US 12 as well. Native Americans were driven down The Saulk Trail as they were forced to leave their land and lifestyle. There was ancestral worship, bootlegging, Al Capone and his gang had several haunts along this road. US 12 has been used for drug trafficking, sex trafficking, and many other sinful behaviors, all of which has left an imprint on the land.

Some may wonder, "what does this have to do with me?" Suppose the travelers along The Saulk Trail, now US 12, spread toxins as they traveled. Would modern travelers be exempt from arsenic or anthrax just because they didn't put it there? Of course not. So why would anyone think they are exempt from curses set in action "caused" by previous generations?

While confessing iniquitous patterns of our ancestors is biblical and helpful, we also need to address the curses caused by what our forefathers did. Curses can be passed down for ten or more generations! As one generation after another walks the same trails of sin and iniquity, they reinforce the impact of curses sin brings upon future generations.

In this study, we will look at seven core curses which began with Adam and Eve's disobedience and have therefore impacted every generation since. Every generation since Adam's has walked similar paths and driven the power of the seven core curses deeper and wider. The curses we face do, indeed, have a cause! Such is the bad news, but there is good news too.

📖 We follow this sequence in Scripture: The First Adam received life, the Last Adam is a life-giving Spirit. Physical life comes first, then spiritual—a firm base shaped from the earth, a final completion coming out of heaven. The First Man was made out of earth, and people since then are earthy; the Second Man was made out of heaven, and people now can be heavenly. In the same way that we've worked from our earthy origins, let's embrace our heavenly ends. 1 Corinthians 15:45-49. The Message.

Jesus is the second and last Adam. The good news, the Gospel of Jesus Christ, shows how Jesus, the second Adam, shed His blood in seven specific places to break seven very powerful curses which have been passed down, gaining strength from generation to generation.

As each of the seven specific core curses is broken through Jesus' blood, seven specific key blessings can be received as we take back to ourselves the blessings Jesus purchased with His blood. Let us work together to apply everything Jesus did for us, not only for our generation but for our descendants also. In Jesus' Name and through the blood of our perfect Passover Lamb. Amen.

TALE OF TWO GARDENS
From Rebellion to Surrender!

There are two very important gardens in Scripture: The Garden of Eden and the Garden of Gethsemane. The Garden of Eden is first mentioned in Genesis 2:8 and is mentioned four other times in Genesis, as well as five other interesting mentions in Isaiah 28:13, Ezekiel 28:13, 31:9, 36:35, and Joel 2:3. The Lord God prepared this garden for Adam and Eve. Adam and Eve were placed in the Garden of Eden and the first garden reveals human life as God intends it to be. The second garden is the Garden of Gethsemane which will be pondered later in this chapter.

📖 The Lord God planted a garden eastward in Eden, and there He put the man whom He had formed. And out of the ground the Lord God made every tree grow that is pleasant to the sight and good for food. The tree of life was also in the midst of the garden, and the tree of the knowledge of good and evil. Genesis 2:8-9.

Adam and Eve enjoyed the fullness of blessing as they communed with the Lord and each other in the Garden of Eden. They lived freely and abundantly, in total absence of curse. They were destined to live forever as they tended the garden for God and ate from the tree of life.

We will look closer at the tree of life and the tree of the knowledge of good and evil more in the addendum at the end of this book. Here we want to consider the full blessing and absence of curse Adam and Eve enjoyed before they sinned. They walked in unashamed transparency with each other and God. There was no rebellion, sin, shame, sickness, iniquity, poverty, natural disaster, or death in the garden. They communicated openly with God, each other, and even with animals. They walked in dominion and authority over the earth.

Their only enemy was the devil, an intruder cast out of heaven to earth. He did his very best to find a way to steal dominion and authority from humans. Somehow he discerned it would be easier to deceive Eve first and then use her to draw Adam into rebellion.

The devil tempted Eve to reject God's sovereignty and to lust after things God wanted to protect her from. The devil deceived her into thinking what she wanted was more important than what God wanted her to have. Take a new look at some familiar Scriptures.

   📖 Now the serpent was more cunning than any beast of the field which the Lord God had made. And he said to the woman, "Has God indeed said, 'You shall not eat of every tree of the garden'?" And the woman said to the serpent, "We may eat the fruit of the trees of the garden; but of the fruit of the tree which *is* in the midst of the garden, God has said, 'You shall not eat it, nor shall you touch it, lest you die.'" Genesis 3:1-2.

Eve didn't appear surprised when a serpent talked with her, but the devil gained an opening when Eve began listening to the devil's contrary voice through the serpent. His spirit was transferred to Eve because she didn't resist that voice. Even though she could quote God's command, the devil had her attention and was quick to divert her focus from God's Word.

   📖 Then the serpent said to the woman, "You will not surely die. For God knows that in the day you eat of it your eyes will be opened, and you will be like God, knowing good and evil." Genesis 3:4-5.

Eve must have thought she could protect herself from deception. Satan crouched at her door, tempting her to think more highly of herself than she should. James outlines the progression from temptation to desire, from desire to sin, and from sin to death which follows the very same pattern as Eve's.

   📖 But each one is tempted when he is drawn away by his own desires and enticed. Then, when desire has conceived, it gives birth to sin; and sin, when it is full-grown, brings forth death. James 1:14-15.

The devil tempted Eve, and she became pregnant with desire which gave birth to sin and led to death.

📖 So when the woman saw that the tree *was* good for food, that it *was* pleasant to the eyes, and a tree desirable to make *one* wise, she took of its fruit and ate. She also gave to her husband with her, and he ate. Genesis 3:6.

In the first garden, Eve was deceived and Adam willingly chose to go along with his wife. Perhaps Adam was more concerned with Eve's approval than God's. For the first time they put selfish desire above God's will for their lives. They grabbed what they wanted instead of surrendering fully to God's command. They did not seek first God's Kingdom and His righteousness. They failed to trust Him to add all things unto them if they would put God first.

I meditated on this thought as I drove to the Branch County Jail to deliver a message on this subject. The thoughts flowed concerning how Eve and Adam chose to: look out for themselves, take care of themselves, protect themselves, please themselves, and put themselves as #1 and God as #2.

In the Garden of Eden, Adam took of the fruit and his actions basically said "Not *thy* will, but *mine* be done." The blessing of obedience was lost at that point and the curse from disobedience fell upon humans. There are 10 major indicators of a curse resulting from disobedience given in passages like Deuteronomy 23:2-3 and 28:15-68. I give a very truncated list of these indicators below. Having any of these indicators in your family line, going back at least three or four generations may indicate you have lived under personal or generational curse of disobedience. I take this list from the Deep Healing and Deliverance Questionnaire I use for personal appointments.

Which of the following issues is part of your family's history in the last 4 generations? (Include adopted family)
☐ Mental and/or emotional breakdown?
☐ Repeated or chronic sicknesses, especially if hereditary?
☐ Barrenness, multiple miscarriages, female problems?
☐ Breakdown of marriage, family problems and alienation?
☐ Ongoing financial problems?
☐ Being "accident prone?"
☐ Suicides, unusual or untimely deaths?
☐ Failure; plans and projects meet with disaster?
☐ Life traumas; going from one crisis to another?

☐ Spiritually hindered in hearing God's voice, sensing His Presence, understanding God's Word, praying or using spiritual gifts?

When I receive completed questionnaires, most people have at least a few of these indicators, while others mark them all. I always share what percentage of the indicators are true of them and mention "that is the bad news, but there is good news too." Jesus shed His blood to give you power to break each curse! Consider the curse Adam brought upon humans in the first Garden. That curse has been passed down from generation to generation. Thankfully, in another garden, the Garden of Gethsemane, Jesus, the "second Adam," sweat drops of blood that fell to the ground of that garden. When He shed that blood, He broke the power of the curse of disobedience in order to redeem the blessing of obedience for mankind. We can apply that blood and be free!

Larry Huch, in his excellent book *"The 7 Places Jesus Shed His Blood,"* first inspired my thinking along these lines. On page 26 of that book he writes:

This is how Jesus shed His blood in the Garden. Medical doctors confirm that at times of intense fear or agony, a person's blood vessels can literally break beneath the skin, and blood will begin to come out of his pores like sweat. Out of Jesus' pores came sweat and blood because of the anxiety or fear, and the turmoil He was experiencing. Why is this significant? We must keep in mind that we've been redeemed by the blood. The first Adam surrendered our willpower to Satan. The second Adam, Jesus, redeemed our willpower by saying "Father, not my will, but Thy will" and sweating great drops of blood. This is where we gain back our willpower to overcome the drug problems, the alcohol problems, the anger problems, and the depression problems.[1]

I spent a weekend musing over why people, including Christians, do what they know is contrary to God's Word and will. Why do Believers look at pornography? Why do they withhold their tithe? Why do they choose anger and hatred when they know God tells them to forgive? Why do they speak evil of leaders or gossip about one another? Why do they choose to do what they feel like doing rather than what God tells them do? I wrote the book *"God's Say So versus Man's Know So"*[2] because I see how many deliverance issues could be avoided if people would simply obey God rather than giving in to personal lusts. Bill Sudduth, leader of the International Society of Deliverance ministers said "There are two ways to get rid of demons, you can starve them out or cast them out." When we learn to simply live obedient lives, demons will not have much to feed on.

I believe God gave me a simple acrostic for the word "sin." I will give you the first word, then the third one, and later add the middle one which sums them all up.

Selfishness: Thinking it is all about ME.
Narcissism: Thinking primarily about self.

I turned to Wikipedia for the definition of narcissism.

From Wikipedia, the free encyclopedia: Main article: History of narcissism: The term "narcissism" comes from the Greek myth of Νάρκισσος, or in Latin Narcissus, a handsome Greek youth who rejected according to Ovid the desperate advances of the nymph Echo. These advances eventually led Narcissus to fall in love with his own reflection in a pool of water. Unable to consummate his love, Narcissus "lay gazing enraptured into the pool, hour after hour," and finally changed into a flower that bears his name, the narcissus.

Wikipedia also gives these traits and signs of narcissism. Our dimensions of narcissism as a personality variable have been delineated: leadership/authority, superiority/ arrogance, self-absorption/self-admiration, and exploitativeness/ entitlement.[3]

Right in the middle of the acrostic "sin" is the letter around which all selfishness and narcissism reigns. More than any other letter it defines the reality of sin. The letter "I" stands for an independent "I" controlled life rather than a God controlled life.

Selfishness: Thinking it is all about ME.
Independence: selfish independence, putting "I" first.
Narcissism: Thinking primarily about self.

In the Garden of Eden, Adam and Eve took things into their own hands. They chose to please self and each other rather than obey God. Their choice caused them to have independent, narcissistic natures, commonly referred to as "the sinful nature." Since Adam, all have sinned and fallen short of the glory of God. This terrible curse affects every person until they break it by applying the blood of Jesus by faith.

Jesus shed His blood in seven specific places to break seven specific curses and release seven specific blessings. The first place he did so was the Garden of Gethsemane.

Jesus was tempted in all ways such as we are, yet was without sin. He was tempted to protect Himself from the weight of the world's sin, His Father's judgement, and the penalty of sin which, I believe included spending an eternity in hell over three days and three nights, which only Jesus could do.

There is only one time when Jesus did not refer to God as "Father." Here he used a more generic term for God "Eli." It was on the cross when He cried out:

📖 And about the ninth hour Jesus cried out with a loud voice, saying, "Eli, Eli, lama sabachthani?" that is, "My God, My God, why have You forsaken Me?" Mathew 27:46.

Imagine the stress of One who said "I and the Father are one," knowing He would soon be separated from Father God. Jesus was tempted to be selfish, independent, and narcissistic. He was tempted to have a self-protective will.

Jesus asked His best friends to stay awake and pray with Him. He warned them to keep watching and praying they not fall into temptation, for the spirit was willing but their flesh was weak. Every one of those friends let Him down. Imagine Jesus' pain. To see the whole story, you need to read about the Garden of Gethsemane from Matthew 26:36-45, Mark 14:32-41, and Luke 22:39-44.

📖 Coming out, He went to the Mount of Olives, as He was accustomed, and His disciples also followed Him. When He came to the place, He said to them, "Pray that you may not enter into temptation." And He was withdrawn from them about a stone's throw, and He knelt down and prayed, saying, "Father, if it is Your will, *take this cup away from Me; nevertheless not My will, but Yours, be done.*" Then an angel appeared to Him from heaven, strengthening Him. And being in agony, He prayed more earnestly. Then *His sweat became like great drops of blood falling down to the ground.* Luke 22:39-44 (Italicized for emphasis).

I find it interesting the word "sweat" is used in only two verses in the Bible. The first is when God told the first Adam "by the sweat of your brow you will eat your food until you return to the ground." The second verse is really interesting because it refers to Jesus, the "second Adam," sweating blood in the Garden of Gethsemane.

(Note: A few translations use "sweat in Ezekiel 44:18 as well, where it simply refers to priests wearing linen so they would not perspire when they entered the inner court). Our focus here, however, is the curse which caused Adam to work the land by the sweat of his brow in Genesis 3:19 and the blood Jesus sweat to break this curse in the verse below.

📖 And being in anguish, he prayed more earnestly, and *his sweat was like drops of blood* falling to the ground. Luke 22:44 NIV (Italicized for emphasis).

Jesus shed His blood in the Garden of Gethsemane to break the power of the curse caused when Adam and Eve chose to be selfish, independent, narcissistic, and self-protective in the Garden of Eden.

Jesus knew what was going to happen to Him. His spirit and His flesh battled against each other, but He won the victory by submitting to the will of the Father. Jesus won the battle, broke the curse, redeemed us, and gave us back our willpower. He did His part; our part is to apply what He did by faith.

What Jesus did when he shed His blood in the Garden of Gethsemane makes it possible for us to break the curse and iniquity of "I centered" lives, and being ruled by the "ruler of the kingdom of the air, the spirit who is now at work in those who are disobedient" (Ephesians 2:2b). Now we can surrender to God by saying "not my will but thine be done."

We can have our willpower restored! I appreciate support groups like Alcoholics Anonymous and Narcotics Anonymous but, according to what Jesus did in Gethsemane, we don't have to introduce ourselves saying "Hello, I am an alcoholic." Instead we say, "Hello, Jesus won my freedom when he sweat drops of blood in Gethsemane. He broke the curse against by will power, and I can say 'No to drugs and alcohol -- not my will, but His be done!'"

When we choose to break the curse of disobedience in our lives, the power of the blood of Jesus will strengthen us, set us free, and empower us to do God's will. When we apply the blood of Jesus and accept His grace, (which gives us the desire and power to do God's will) the curse of disobedience is broken and our sovereign wills can be fully surrendered to Christ and be restored -- Hallelujah!

Many people, when hurt, build self-protective walls around their hearts. Countless people have been hurt or abused by others. They fear being hurt again, and may feel God has let them down. They tend to hold everyone, including Jesus, at a distance.

Thankfully, Jesus' sweat drops of blood not only broke the curse of a selfish and self-protective will, but also released a blessing of restoration of the willpower to do God's perfect will. This is huge. This means dieters can curb their appetites! Addicts can overcome their addictions. People who know they should read the Bible, pray, and fellowship, will have the willpower to do so, once they invoke the blessing of restored willpower. Paul spoke of this in Philippians 2:13. I share it in a few translations so you can receive the fullness of hope it brings.

📖 For it is [not your strength, but it is] God who is effectively at work in you, *both to will* and *to work* [that is, strengthening, energizing, and creating in you the longing and the ability to fulfill your purpose] for His good pleasure. Philippians 2:13 AMP (Italicized for emphasis).

📖 For it is God who works in you *to will* and *to act* in order to fulfill his good purpose. Philippians 2:13 NIV (Italicized for Italicized for emphasis).

📖 for it is God who works in you both *the willing* and *the working* according to [his] good pleasure. Philippians 2:13 Darby (Italicized for emphasis).

📖 for it is God who works in you both *to will* and *to do* for His good pleasure. Philippians 2:13 (Italicized for emphasis).

Do you understand the promise of this blessing? Your will can be restored to will what God wills! Therefore, His commands are no longer burdensome. As Augustine reportedly said "Love God, and do what you please." He wasn't advocating permissiveness, but expounding on the teaching of Jesus who said "If you love me, you will obey me" (John

14:15). Jesus so loved the Father He fully surrendered His personal will in order to complete the Father's will through Gethsemane and Calvary. Jesus already did His part. It is time for us to partner with Him in doing our part.

Jesus overcame the temptations to be self-centered and to self-protect in Gethsemane. Only Dr. Luke, a physician who wrote the books of Luke and Acts, mentions the sweat drops of blood. It is possible for humans, under great stress, to sweat blood; it is called Hematidrosis.

Hematidrosis (also called hematohidrosis) is a very rare condition in which a human being sweats blood. It may occur when a person is suffering extreme levels of stress, for example, facing his or her own death.

> According to Dr. Frederick Zugibe (Chief Medical Examiner of Rockland County, New York) it is well-known, and there have been many cases of it. The clinical term is "hematohidrosis." "Around the sweat glands, there are multiple blood vessels in a net-like form." Under the pressure of great stress, the vessels constrict. Then as the anxiety passes "the blood vessels dilate to the point of rupture. The blood goes into the sweat glands." As the sweat glands are producing a lot of sweat, it pushes the blood to the surface - coming out as droplets of blood mixed with sweat.[5]

In the Garden of Eden, the first human sin of putting selfish will ahead of God's will invoked a heavy curse against the world and all those in it. Adam sweat for the first time under the heavy burden of working land full of thorns and thistles. In the Garden of Gethsemane, on the other hand, Jesus surrendered all to the Father in the face of agonizing trauma which caused him to sweat drops of blood.

The blood Jesus sweat in Gethsemane has the power to break every curse of selfish, rebellious, or self-protective wills. As we apply His blood to break that curse, we can also invoke the blessing of restored willpower so we have the "will and the to do" God's perfect will.

I suggest invoking Abba Father, in the Name of Jesus, to break the first curse and release the first blessing. A helpful prayer is offered below to assist you in doing just that. It is important you pray in faith and not just hope. Believe God is doing what you ask for as you apply Jesus' blood personally. When you are done breaking curses and invoking blessings, there is a prayer to cast out demons that may have been empowered against you through the curse. Each time you will see the word expel at the end of deliverance I encourage you to resist the devil and his demons by blowing, coughing or yawning so they will flee.

James 4:7 promises if we resist the devil he will flee! The best way I have found to resist the devil through prayers of deliverance is to cough, blow, or yawn in faith, knowing they have to flee when you so resist.

Breaking the Curse and Invoking the Blessing:

⸸ I declare I am redeemed by the blood of the Lamb out of the hand of the enemy!

⸸ Heavenly Father, I invoke You, in the Name of Jesus, to hear and answer my prayer this day.

⸸ Dear Jesus, thank you for resisting the temptation to think about yourself or protect yourself in the Garden.

⸸ Thank you for not throwing in the towel and falling asleep with your best friends.

⸸ Thank you for breaking the curse of Selfishness, Independence, and Narcissism by saying "nevertheless not My will, but Yours, be done."

⸸ Right now Father, I ask You to take the blood Jesus sweat in the Garden of Gethsemane and break the curse of a selfish, self-protective, and rebellious will from my life.

⸸ I invoke Your blessing of absolute abandonment to Abba Father's will.

⸸ I invoke the blessing of Your working in me both to will and to do Your perfect will.

⸸ All to Jesus, I surrender, all to Him I freely give.

⸸ Take my life and let it be, consecrated fully, Lord to Thee.

⸸ Now, in the Name and through the blood of Jesus, I command every demon which was empowered by this curse against my will, to loose me right now.

⸸ I cast you out and command you to go to the feet of Jesus Now! (Expel)

Endnotes:

[1]Larry Huch, *The 7 Places Jesus Shed His Blood.* Whitaker House, 2000, 2004, pg 26.
[2]Douglas Carr, *God's Say So Versus Man's Know So.* Create Space, 2015
[3]Wikipedia, the free encyclopedia.
[4]Dictionary.com
[5]Source(s):http://en.wikipedia.org/wiki/Hematidrosi...
http://answers.google.com/answers/thread...

(Scriptures referred to but not quoted chapter and verse in this chapter include: Mark 15:15-18; John 10:30; Matthew 26:36-45; Mark 14:32-41; Luke 22:39-46.)

HEALING THROUGH HIS STRIPES
From Infirmity to Health!

Adam and Eve were created in the image of God by the hand of God. In His image, they were to live forever. The first Adam, however, brought a curse of death and disease upon the human race. Jesus, the second Adam, came to redeem mankind from the curse of disease and death. Jesus has redeemed those who believe on Him from spiritual death and soon will redeem the faithful from physical death. Paul wrote that the last enemy to be destroyed is death (1 Corinthians 15:26).

Isaiah 53 tells of Jesus' mission to redeem mankind from curses brought by Adam, including disease. Do you think there will be sickness in heaven? I don't. Jesus said "the Kingdom of God is with you" (Luke 17:21). Do you honestly believe sickness has to be part of those walking in the Kingdom of God on earth here and now? It is unfortunate how some Christians, including wonderful servants of the Kingdom, suffer illness and disease and do not even resist it.

There are times when sickness is a direct result of sin. One example comes from the Israelites when they wandered in the desert. They had a "woe is me" attitude and blamed God for problems of their own making. We are often likewise tempted. Some people ignore their need to exercise but blame God for heart disease. Others eat sweets and carbohydrates like they are going out of style yet blame God for diabetes. The same can be said about smoking and lung disease, heavy drinking and kidney disease, or promiscuity and sexually transmitted disease.

The Israelites complained about their circumstances. They didn't like their food, lodging, leadership, or the water quality and quantity. Their complaints turned into blaming God for their situation, and He sent fiery serpents among the people. As you read the Scripture below I believe you will agree the people brought God's judgment upon themselves.

📖 Then they journeyed from Mount Hor by the Way of the Red Sea, to go around the land of Edom; and *the soul of the people became very discouraged* on the way. And the people spoke against God and against Moses: "Why have you brought us up out of Egypt to die in the wilderness? For there is no food and no water, and our soul loathes this worthless bread." So the Lord sent fiery serpents among the people, and they bit the people; and many of the people of Israel died. Numbers 21:4-6 (Italicized for emphasis).

Notice it was the soul of *the people* which became very discouraged. This was more than individual discouragement, it affected the soul of the corporate mass. Sin and wrong thinking often work like this -- they discourage entire groups of people as they are led astray and bound by discouragement or depression. These groups may consist of families, cultures, or even denominations.

A few years ago the Lord arranged for me to meet with several adult children of Holocaust survivors within a period of just a few weeks. Definite patterns were soon apparent as it became clear not one of them felt they had a right to exist. Even though these children of Holocaust survivors did not all know each other, they shared unique patterns as a people group, including self-defeating behaviors. Their collective soul suffered and needed Jesus' healing.

Similar traits are seen in family lines where several generations put up with inherited physical problems from obesity to ovarian cancer, heart disease to overall health, diabetes to diverticulosis and the like. Such diseases can so become the norm in a family line that no one even resists them. They may complain and murmur about their problems but fail to take any physical or spiritual steps to solve their problems.

The Lord judged the Israelites for their self-pity and murmuring. They said there was no food even though God gave them daily portions of mana. It wasn't that they didn't have anything to eat, but they loathed what they called "worthless bread." Rather than being grateful for God's provision, they grumbled. It was their own fault they wandered in the desert forty years. God wanted to lead them in, but their rebellion caused them to wander in the desert.

It is sad when people are stuck in ruts that cause generations to follow similar patterns of defeat, including family diseases. Such sinful thought patterns become cycles of sickness.

God's mercy is evident, however. Even though the Israelites sinned and God released judgment through venomous snakes, God released forgiveness and healing when the people confessed their sin.

📖 Therefore the people came to Moses, and said, "We have sinned, for we have spoken against the Lord and against you; pray to the Lord that He take away the serpents from us." So Moses prayed for the people. Then the Lord said to Moses, *"Make a fiery serpent, and set it on a pole; and it shall be that everyone who is bitten, when he looks at it, shall live."* So Moses made a bronze serpent, and put it on a pole; and so it was, if a serpent had bitten anyone, when he looked at the bronze serpent, he lived. Numbers 21:7-9 (Italicized for emphasis).

The people confessed their sin and the Lord provided a remedy for their sin *and* sickness. Some might think, "but that's Old Testament." In the New Testament, however, we discover the deeper meaning of the bronze snake which pointed to Jesus' death. The New Testament is in the Old Testament concealed, and the Old Testament is in the New Testament revealed, as seen in John chapter three.

📖 No one has ascended to heaven but He who came down from heaven, that is, the Son of Man who is in heaven. And *as Moses lifted up the serpent in the wilderness,* even so must *the Son of Man be lifted up,* that whoever believes in Him should not perish but have eternal life. John 3:13-15 (Italicized for emphasis).

The curse of sickness and death came through Adam's disobedience. Deuteronomy 28 outlines God's blessings upon the obedient and their children. It also lists corresponding illnesses, including the diseases of the Egyptians who worshiped false gods, which would come upon the disobedient and their children.

📖 If you do not carefully follow all the words of this law, which are written in this book, and do not revere this glorious and awesome name--the LORD your God--the LORD will send fearful plagues on you and your descendants, harsh and prolonged disasters, and severe and lingering illnesses. He will bring upon you all the diseases of Egypt that you dreaded, and they will cling to you. The LORD will also *bring on you every kind of sickness* and disaster not recorded in this Book of the Law, until you are destroyed. Deuteronomy 28:58-61 NIV (Italicized for emphasis).

As a side note, whenever you see "LORD" in all capital letters, it refers to God the Father's proper name, "Jehovah" which means "I am that I am." (Which helps one understand why the Scribes and Pharisees were so enraged when Jesus used "I am" statements like "I am the bread of life.") Jehovah gave His only begotten Son as a perfect sacrifice to redeem us from all sin and every curse, including the curse of sickness, whether physical, mental, or emotional.

Visualize, if you can, Jesus' bleeding back. Picture His stripes, bruises and bleeding. There is a healing evangelist who prays "by the stripes on Jesus' back, you are healed!" That's what the Bible says! Peter seems to misquote Isaiah because Isaiah says "we *are* healed," while Peter says "we *were* healed." Compare the next two scriptures. Isaiah wrote:

📖 But He was wounded for our transgressions, He was bruised for our iniquities; The chastisement for our peace was upon Him, and by His stripes we *are* healed. Isaiah 53:5 (Italicized for emphasis).

📖 Who Himself bore our sins in His own body on the tree, that we, having died to sins, might live for righteousness—by whose stripes you *were* healed. I Peter 2:24 (Italicized for emphasis).

Since all Scripture was inspired as people were "carried along by the Holy Spirit" (2 Peter 1:21), we can ask Holy Spirit about seeming contradictions like "are" in Isaiah and "were" in 1 Peter. When I asked Him about this He said, "Isaiah was looking forward to the cross by faith and wrote "*are* healed." Peter was looking back at the cross and was inspired to write "by his stripes you *were* healed."

We live on this side of the cross and we can apply the blood Jesus shed so many years ago to our physical needs now for healing.

Recently the Lord dropped a phrase into my spirit, which became the main title of this book: "I want to transform every *'Woe is Me" to "Wow is HE."* I shared this with our congregation one Sunday and the following week people testified for 25 minutes how God had transitioned their "Woe is me" to "Wow is HE." Jesus already shed His blood for our healing. He did His part and now we need to do ours by applying His blood by faith to our needs. We need to diligently pursue the transition from *"Woe is me to Wow is He!"*

One third of the healings in the New Testament included deliverance. Jesus delivered a woman from a spirit of infirmity who had been crippled and bent over for 18 years (Luke 13:10-13). A spirit of infirmity is a result of the curse, but Jesus shed His blood so every born again believer can be redeemed from the curse!

Jesus paid the price for our healing through the blood which poured from the stripes on His back. When Christians have sickness, the devil is trespassing and we need to tell him to stop. We can *apply* what Jesus did to what the devil is trying to do, and make the devil stop!

As if to underscore what God wants me to share, I was tempted to give into sickness the night before proofing this! Even though my wife and I have not had stomach flu for decades, I went to bed concerned for a friend who was suffering from the stomach flu. I had gone to bed before 9:00, exhausted from overdoing it for a few weeks. I woke at 10:45 pm feeling quite sick. I went into the bathroom feeling like I would feel better if only I gave into the sickness. Thankfully, Holy Spirit reminded me to resist the temptation to be sick. Within a few minutes I felt fine, went back to bed and slept nearly an hour longer than usual!

Jesus still heals, He still wants to heal! But healing comes through *applying* the blood from the stripes on His back by faith. His blood was shed so we can be redeemed from *every* sickness and disease.

I used to pray for healing based on the wrong religious thinking it might be God's will for His blood-bought children to continue suffering physically. I believed in the power of God to heal, but didn't realize His work for healing was fully completed on the Cross. I used to end every prayer for healing with the words "if it be thy will," thus giving my faith an out in case healing didn't come. Healing seldom came and my family and I endured yearly bouts with the flu, colds, sinus problems and the like. Thankfully, since 1995, we have learned we have the right to resist sickness just as we have the right to resist the devil. We no longer suffer all the sicknesses we used to suffer.

We used to get intestinal flu at least once a year, complete with high fever, vomiting, and the whole works. Now we resist it if we feel it trying to come. I have only vomited once since 1995 after we learned to spiritually resist sickness, and that was after a deliverance from Free Masonry. My wife didn't even have to experience that. Now we resist the spirit of infirmity when it tries to attack.

A spirit of infirmity is often present where there is a high fever. For years I carried an instant read thermometer when I prayed for the sick, especially children. Time and again a child's fever would instantly drop from a high fever to normal after we rebuked the spirit of infirmity. But we didn't pray "if it is your will." Instead we told that spirit of infirmity to go in Jesus' Name and through His blood.

Jesus was flogged mercilessly with a whip embedded with metal and bone. Jewish law allowed forty lashes but they usually stopped at 39 because forty lashes often caused death. I've read there are 39 broad categories of disease. Others say there are 39 root causes of diseases. If either of those ideas are true, then Jesus took one stripe for each category of disease. As I spent just a little time researching this idea I found one web posting that said "Yes, just recently in 2010 there was a reclassification from 17 to 39 broad categories!" What an awesome God we serve!"

I have not been able to do enough research to substantiate there are 39 broad categories of disease. That truly is an exciting idea -- but I find another idea in the Scriptures more exciting. Matthew tells how Jesus healed all their sick. It doesn't matter if there are 39 categories of disease or 390, Jesus is our Great Physician and Healer!

📖 Aware of this, Jesus withdrew from that place. Many followed him, and *he healed all their sick*. Matthew 12:15 NIV (Italicized for emphasis).

I love the word "all" here. Someone said "All means all and that's all 'all' means!" Do you believe Jesus still wants to heal "all the sick?" Some schools of Christianity teach Jesus doesn't heal today like He did while He was on earth. Most of these schools believe the Bible is the Word of God, so I cannot understand how they can teach contrary to what Scripture says.

📖 Jesus Christ is the same yesterday and today and forever. Hebrews 13:8 NIV.

Jesus healed yesterday and He heals today! His blood was already shed and by His stripes we were healed. All we have to do is appropriate His blood!

Remember, Jesus shed His blood in seven specific places to break seven specific curses and release specific blessings. We, however, need to apply what He did by breaking every curse by faith and invoking blessings. Let me help you do so on the next page.

Breaking the Curse and Invoking the Blessing:

- I declare I am redeemed by the blood of the Lamb out of the hand of the enemy!
- In Jesus' Name I apply the blood from the stripes on Jesus' bleeding back to my health!
- I break the curse of sickness, disease, and dis-ease and command the spirit of infirmity to leave me now in Jesus' name. (expel!)
- I break every ancestral curse of specific illnesses seen in my family line including . . . (mention specific chronic illnesses in your family line).
- Devil, I apply the blood from Jesus' stripes and command you to stop trespassing in my life! (Resist through blowing!)
- Jesus, I receive my healing by faith!
- Father, in the Mighty Name of Jesus and through the power of His blood, I invoke Your blessing that none of the diseases of the Egyptians will be upon me.
- I invoke Your blessing I will prosper in all things even as my soul prospers, in Jesus' Name. Amen.
- I receive the blessing of good health.
- Now, in the Name and through the blood of Jesus, I command every demon which was empowered by this curse against my will, to loose me right now.
- I cast you out and command you to go to the feet of Jesus Now! (Expel)

TAKING BACK FREEDOM THROUGH HIS BRUISES
From Bondage to Freedom!

Why do you think you, or perhaps those you work with, continue doing negative things which hinder them from reaching their goals, hurt those they love, and/or give the enemy openings to kill, steal, and destroy? What is the underlying force which compels people to turn back to addictions which destroy, relationships which cause pain, or lifestyles that always disappoint? Could it be there is an underlying pattern that tugs at people to repeat destructive behaviors? Are there things working beneath the surface that sabotage our best plans and desires?

The first Adam and his wife were created without sin. They, however, gave into sin and iniquity entered which passed down generationally to the point one of their own sons killed his brother! Iniquitous patterns are not only passed down generationally, but are also reinforced as people continue giving in to them.

Have you ever had a bruise or blood blister? Remember how badly it hurt? Have you banged your finger or stubbed your toe, and had a blood blister under a fingernail or toenail? These are called "subungual hematomas" and are more painful than open wounds. Small subungual hematomas usually require no treatment. However, the pressure generated by pooled blood under the nail can be extremely painful. To relieve the pain, a doctor may perform decompression, also called trephination, which allows the underlying blood to drain, relieving pressure and pain to the area.

Many people have spiritual and emotional "subungual hematomas." These always require treatment by the Great Physician; without His intervention the pain and pressure remain. I'm referring, of course, to deep inner pain people carry from ancestral or personal wounds, trauma, heartache, and/or iniquitous patterns. Such pain runs deep, often remains hidden, but the pain and pressure remain until Jesus is invited to do His healing work.

Physical bruising is evidence of inner bleeding. The blood flows beneath the surface of the skin. We already considered how Jesus sweat drops of blood to break the curse of a narcissistic and/or self-protective will. We studied how to break the curse of infirmity and walk in health through the stripes on Jesus' back. Now we turn to how Jesus' blood was shed through bruising to free us from inner pain and the curse of iniquity. Consider what Isaiah prophesied centuries before the incarnate Jesus dwelt among men.

📖 Surely He has borne our griefs and carried our sorrows; Yet we esteemed Him stricken, smitten by God, and afflicted. But He was wounded for our transgressions, *He was bruised for our iniquities*; The chastisement for our peace was upon Him, and by His stripes we are healed. All we like sheep have gone astray; We have turned, every one, to his own way; *And the Lord has laid on Him the iniquity of us all.* Isaiah 53:4-6 (Italicized for emphasis).

We need to take a deeper look at the word "iniquity." Jesus was bruised for our iniquities. The Lord, Jehovah, laid on Jesus the iniquity of us all. Unfortunately, many Bibles translate the Hebrew word for iniquity as sin. Rather than doing a rewrite on this I take the following long quote from my book "*Getting to the Dirty Rotten Inner Core.*"[1]

We understand that the sins of the parents are visited to the third and fourth generation but we need to look a little deeper -- the word translated "sin(s)" in many Bibles is more accurately translated iniquities ("avon" from the Hebrew) or faults ("paraptoma" from the Greek).

Iniquity defines the bent, perversity or patterns of ungodly or faithless behaviors like addictions, depression, entitlement thinking, victimization, and the like.

According to the above definition I believe all will agree that rage and anger are ungodly behaviors. Consider a well-known verse from Exodus.

📖 Thou shalt not bow down thyself unto them, nor serve them, for I Jehovah thy God am a jealous God, *visiting the iniquity* of the fathers upon the children, upon the third and upon the fourth generation of them that hate me, and showing loving-kindness unto thousands of them that love me and keep my commandments. Exodus 20:5-6 ASV (Italicized for emphasis).

Iniquity (avon): describes crookedness or perverseness; a moral distortion. It refers to the bent, perversity or pattern that affects generations and land.

Iniquity describes the character flaw behind the action of sin.

The word iniquity describes the character behind the action or sin. It is incorrect to use "sin" as a synonym of iniquity.

The Hebrew word is "avon'" and is rightly translated iniquity 220 times in the King James Version. It is defined as:

1) Perversity, depravity, iniquity, guilt or punishment of iniquity
1a) iniquity
1b) guilt of iniquity, guilt (as great), guilt (of condition)
1c) consequence of or punishment for iniquity.[2]

"Avon'" comes from the word "avah" which is translated: iniquity 4, perverse 2, perversely 2, perverted 2, amiss 1, turn 1, crooked 1, bowed down 1, troubled 1, wickedly 1, and wrong 1. It is defined as:

1) to bend, twist, distort
1a) (Niphal) to be bent, be bowed down, be twisted, be perverted
1b) (Piel) to twist, distort
1c) (Hiphil) to do perversely
2) to commit iniquity, do wrong, pervert
2a) (Qal) to do wrong, commit iniquity.[2]

📖 But we are all as an unclean [thing], and all our righteousnesses [are] as filthy rags; *(Used menstrual cloth – sign of infertility)* and we all do fade as a leaf; and our iniquities, *(Avon: bent, distortion, twisting or perversion)* like the wind, have taken us away. And [there is] none that calleth upon thy name, that stirreth up himself to take hold of thee: for thou hast hid thy face from us, and hast consumed us, because of our iniquities. Isaiah 64:6-7 KJV (words italicized in parentheses are mine).

Have you heard people say somebody is a "chip off the old block?" Or "for better or worse, he is just like his father," or sayings like "like father, like son," "like mother, like daughter," etc.? When such statements are true in a negative sense, it is the work of generational iniquities or as it says in the Hebrew "avon." Avon's line of personal care products used to be advertised on television with sharp looking sales personal visiting and saying "Ding-dong, Avon Calling. Understanding the Hebrew meaning of "avon" brings a whole new meaning to "ding-dong, avon calling!"

When you visit a doctor the first thing they ask you to do is fill out a family history. Medical conditions in the family line set a pattern for the same in the descendants. In deep healing we do the same thing, but also focus on iniquitous patterns of behavior, or spiritual sickness, rather than merely physical conditions. Praise the Lord! All is not lost! Jesus came to destroy every work of the devil! (1 John 3:8) He wants to break those generational patterns of iniquities and the power of generational curses -- and He will -- if we do it HIS way. But first, let's look at the Greek word that is best translated "faults" but often mistranslated "sins."

"Faults" is defined as: fall away, deviate from right path, fall under judgment and come under condemnation.

Let me share how New Testament Greek sheds light on this:
3895 parapipto par-ap-ip'-to} AV - fall away 1 = 1) to fall beside
   a person or thing, 2) to slip aside,
   2a) to deviate from the right path, turn aside, wander
   2b) to error
   2c) to fall away (from the true faith): from worship of
   Jehovah
From root "pipto":
AV - fall 69, fall down 19, light 1, fail 1; 90
   1) to descend from a higher place to a lower
   1a) to fall (either from or upon)
   1a1) to be thrust down
   1b) metaph. to fall under judgment, came under
   condemnation
   2) to descend from an erect to a prostrate position
   2a1) to be prostrated, fall prostrate
   2a2) of those overcome by terror or astonishment or grief or
   under the attack of an evil spirit or of falling dead suddenly
   2a3) the dismemberment of a corpse by decay.[2]

I trust you have been patient while I have explained all this. The Bible gives specific instructions on being healed of generation curses and faults.

We have missed something terribly important by a wrong translation of James 5:16. In the Bible program I use, several versions wrongly translate this word as I believe the NIV does.

📖 Therefore confess your *sins* to each other and pray for each other so that you may be healed. The prayer of a righteous man is powerful and effective. James 5:16 NIV (Italicized for emphasis).

A few versions in Bible Gateway translate the Greek correctly, in my opinion, as the King James Version does.

📖 Confess [your] *faults* one to another, and pray one for another, that ye may be healed. The effectual fervent prayer of a righteous man availeth much. James 5:16 KJV (Italicized for emphasis).

James 5:16 tells us to go deep beneath the surface to deal with iniquity. It isn't enough to confess "I was mad at my spouse." We are encouraged to get to the root of the issue by confessing "I am an angry person," or "I really struggle with anger." We are to move beyond saying "I looked at pornography," and get to the root by saying "I am consumed with lust," or whatever the problem may be.

There is a curse working behind ongoing sinful patterns, especially when those patterns have flowed generationally. These patterns may include stinking thinking, depression, wrong responses to life, as well as addictions, promiscuity, covenant breaking, etc. As we confess our faults to one another, we can receive prayer from those who have overcome such faults and be healed! Imagine what will happen as a person struggling with pornography or addiction confesses those faults and iniquities, and receives prayer from someone who has overcome those things! Spiritual, emotional, and relational victory will be won when we break the curse of iniquity and receive prayer concerning personal faults. This is body-life as Jesus intended it to be!

So let's consider how Jesus was bruised for our iniquities. When skin puffs up and turns purple or black and blue, it means the pain inflicted has caused bleeding underneath the skin. There are people all around us who are bruised, broken and bleeding on the inside. Outside they may act tough or paste on a smile, dress up nice and look invincible. Inside, however, there may be multiple fragments of hurting and wounded identities.

One of my greatest joys in ministering deep healing is when people invite Jesus to show them where He was and what He was doing when they went through horrible times of abuse or trauma. They often recognize Jesus was there either shielding them from further damage, or bearing their shame and pain for them.

Recently a woman who had been raped by her much older brother when she was a very young child, asked Jesus where He was when her brother did that to her. The Holy Spirit gave her a picture of Jesus entering her broken heart. As she recognized Jesus was there and that He does care, she was able to receive healing for her inner brokenness.

Isaiah prophesied Jesus bore our grief and carried our sorrows. He was wounded for our transgressions. But then he goes a little deeper and says that Jesus was bruised for our iniquities. Let me remind you, "iniquities" refer to personal or generational patterns of perversity, shame, guilt, bent or twisted inner character.

Iniquity is deeper than sin, it is character traits from which the actions of sin spring forth. Jesus was bruised, He bled on the inside to break the power of the curse of inner iniquity, which often rules as fruit borne by inner pain and deep inner wounds. Jesus was bruised for our sake so we can overcome both the inner bruising, and the iniquitous character we have developed or inherited.

The good news is Jesus was bruised for our iniquity. Some of His precious blood flowed underneath the surface of His skin, hidden from sight, but powerful to break the curse of iniquity.

This is almost too wonderful to proclaim. Jesus paid it all, all to him I owe, sin had left a crimson stain, He washed it white as snow. *Jesus' bruises heal our pain from deep inner wounds and iniquity!*

We know and sing truths of the Gospel, but they do not become personal reality until we intentionally apply the blood to break the curse of iniquity. The descendants of addicts are prone to addiction. The descendants of divorced parents or grandparents are prone to covenant-breaking. The descendants of people who rely on government to supply all their needs are often given to entitlement thinking. The children and grandchildren of people who were sexually promiscuous or given to crime are often subject to similar iniquitous patterns. Such is the bad news of iniquity being passed down to the third and fourth generation.

The good news, however, is Jesus was bruised for our iniquity! Some of His precious blood flowed underneath the surface of His skin, hidden from sight, but powerful to break the curse of iniquity.

It is helpful to be specific in applying the blood from Jesus' bruises to explicit personal and generational iniquitous patterns. For example, if someone has always given in to a "poor me" spirit, apply the blood from Jesus' bruises to break the iniquitous curse of the "poor me" spirit. The same applies to iniquitous patterns of anger, depression, bitterness, self-rejection, condemnation or any other bent or distortion of character which leads to defeat. Once you have broken definite curses of iniquity you can prepare to invoke blessings.

Jesus not only shed his blood to break every curse and to set the captive free -- He also died, was buried and rose from the dead to give us the Power of His Resurrection to walk out everything He did for us. Paul exhorts to become like Jesus!

📖 I want to know Christ and the power of his resurrection and the fellowship of sharing in his sufferings, *becoming like him* in his death, and so, somehow, to attain to the resurrection from the dead. Philippians 3:10-11 NIV (Italicized for emphasis).

I pray these thoughts will be engrafted in your soul over the next days and weeks. Holy Spirit will reveal one issue at a time until we are conformed to the image of Christ!

Before praying to break curses of iniquity and invoke blessings of holiness and victory, I challenge you to soak in the Holy Spirit for a few moments and jot down specific personal or generational patterns of perversity, shame, guilt, bent or twisted inner character so you can address them in the prayer which will follow your list.

_____
_____
_____
_____
_____
_____
_____
_____
_____
_____
_____
_____

Breaking the Curse and Invoking the Blessing:

☦ Jesus, I need You and Your bondage-breaking power.
☦ I declare I am redeemed from iniquity by the blood of the Lamb out of the hand of the enemy!
☦ I put my faith in You and receive You as Savior, Lord, Deliverer, and Protector.
☦ In Jesus' Name I apply the blood from Your bruises to break every curse of iniquity, and bent or distortion of character from my life.
☦ I have specific areas of iniquity in my life and in the lives of my ancestors, so I now confess them one by one . . . (Confess from the preceding list).
☦ Father God, I ask you to apply the blood from Jesus' bruises to break every curse of iniquity in my family line, including . . . (list specific iniquitous patterns).
☦ Now, because of what Jesus for me, I invoke Your blessing of holiness and freedom from personal and generational iniquity from me and my children.
☦ I command every personal or ancestral demon working to keep me bound to iniquitous patterns to release me now in the Name and through the blood of Jesus. (Expel)
☦ In the powerful Name of Jesus Christ. Amen.

Endnotes Chapter Four:
[1]Carr, Douglas Getting to the Dirty Rotten Inner Core, Create Space 2014.   Pages 18-22.
[2]Strong, James. S.T.D, LL.D. Strong's Exhaustive Concordance of the Bible. The Old-Time Gospel Hour Edition.

TAKING HOLD OF PROSPERITY
From Poverty to Prosperity!

The Lord dropped some questions into my spirit while I was prayer-walking. I was meditating on Jesus' crown of thorns and God placed some things on my heart. I truly want everyone who reads this to receive this truth and live it out. I want you to prosper and be the head and not the tail. I want you to get out of debt, prepare a nest egg, and prosper. Here are the questions the Lord wants you to consider and answer:

➤ Do you want to be poor or prosperous?

➤ Do you want to barely make it, often paying late fees on your bills, or have enough money to pay all your bills on time, and money left over to liberally bless your family and others?

➤ Do you want to walk in blessing and abundance with the floodgates of heaven open over you; or are you OK letting the Devourer hold you back and corrupt or steal your wealth?

➤ Do you want to live by faith -- grateful how God supplies all your needs according to His riches in Christ Jesus -- or do you want to live by mooch – depending on the government or others to supply your basic needs?

➤ Do you want to leave an inheritance for your children, or leave them the burden of scrapping up money for your final care?

➤ In short, do you want to break the curse of poverty over your life and invoke the blessing of prosperity?

I realize those who read this come from various circumstances. Some already walk in the blessing of prosperity. Others are retired and hope the money they put into Social Security and other investments will be enough. Some are disabled and unable to work. God's truths, however, apply to all people in all situations. As someone said years ago, "God's work, done God's way, will never lack God's resources." Such is true of individuals and ministries. Jesus became poor for our sakes so through His poverty we might become rich through Him. Do you really believe that?

📖 For you know the grace of our Lord Jesus Christ, that though he was rich, yet for your sake he became poor, *so that you through his poverty might become rich.* 2 Corinthians 8:9 NIV (Italicized for emphasis).

In the fall of 2014 my wife and I downsized from a large house on over eleven acres to a small one on one acre. We obeyed some prophetic words which affirmed what we already sensed, that we will become so busy there won't be time to take care of the home, property, and animals we had enjoyed for seventeen years.

We had an auction to liquidate the overabundance of possessions we had and still had to take over a dozen truckloads of clothing and housewares to donate to Good Will. It was quite painful to go through the process of downsizing, even though we knew the Lord wanted us to. We had to "give a lot of things up."

Can you imagine how much Jesus had to downsize when He emptied Himself, left the glory of heaven, and came to earth to be born in a stable? I like the way the Amplified Bible elaborates this.

📖 For you are recognizing [more clearly] the grace of our Lord Jesus Christ [His astonishing kindness, His generosity, His gracious favor], *that though He was rich, yet for your sake He became poor, so that by His poverty you might become rich* (abundantly blessed). 2 Corinthians 8:9 AMP (Italicized for emphasis).

Let's dig deeper into Jesus' crown of thorns, and how to use His blood from the thorns to break the curse of poverty. We've all seen pictures and movies about the Passion Week of Jesus. We've seen the crown of thorns pressed into the skin around his forehead. But there is more to that story and it starts back in the Garden of Eden.

📖 To Adam he said, "Because you listened to your wife and ate from the tree about which I commanded you, `You must not eat of it,' "*Cursed is the ground because of you; through painful toil* you will eat of it all the days of your life. *It will produce thorns and thistles for you*, and you will eat the plants of the field. *By the sweat of your brow* you will eat your food until you return to the ground, since from it you were taken; for dust you are and to dust you will return." Genesis 3:17-19 NIV.

God cursed the land in judgment of sin, and work became increasingly difficult. Work in itself is not a curse. Adam worked the garden before he fell and God released the corresponding curse. As we will see later, the curse came against the ease, fruitfulness, and profitability of work. The curse on the woman's labor of childbirth, robbed her of the joy and ease of bearing children.

The Bible shows work as a blessing and an obligation. We are supposed to work hard, provide for ourselves and our families, and support the work of the Kingdom. Paul says people who are unwilling to work, fail to live out their faith!

📖 *Anyone who does not provide for their relatives*, and especially for their own household, has denied the faith and *is worse than an unbeliever.* 1 Timothy 5:8 NIV (Italicized for emphasis).

Part of our Christian duty is to work with our own hands and be as independent financially as we can be. While taking care of the poor and generosity are commended in the Bible, entitlement thinking is forbidden. Paul stresses godly independence.

📖 Yet we urge you, brothers and sisters, to do so more and more, and to make it your ambition to lead a quiet life: You should mind your own business and *work with your hands*, just as we told you, so that your daily life may win the respect of outsiders and *so that you will not be dependent on anybody.* 1 Thessalonians 4:10b-12 NIV (Italicized for emphasis).

There were some people in Thessalonica who felt they were entitled to take advantage of the generosity of others rather than earning their own keep, just as there is in our day. Paul gives this strong word.

📖 For even when we were with you, we gave you this rule: "*The one who is unwilling to work shall not eat.*" We hear that some among you are idle and disruptive. They are not busy; they are busybodies. Such people we command and urge in the Lord Jesus Christ to *settle down and earn the food they eat.* 2 Thessalonians 3:10-12 NIV (Italicized for emphasis).

I heard a true story of an older woman whose adult son still lived with her. The woman worked very hard, but her son seldom held down a job for more than a few weeks. Even though she was well past retirement age, she wouldn't even consider quitting her job because she wouldn't receive enough retirement benefits to take of her and her son. Her friends tried to convince her she should retire and let her son learn to get a job and earn his keep.

God finally used the woman's waning strength to convince her it was time to retire. The next day when her son woke up he noticed his mother was still home. He yelled at her, saying, "Mom, you are going to be late for work," to which she replied, "I finally retired, I am not going to work." He couldn't believe it, but the next day she was still at home so he asked "How are we going to have money for groceries and rent?" She said "I don't know, I trust the Lord will take care of me, but I don't know about you."

After a few days of wondering how his mother would be able to take care of their needs without working, the son decided to do something about it. He was gone the next day when his mother woke up and didn't return home until late in the day. His mother asked him where he had been all day and he replied "I went to look for a job and I start tomorrow!" There are times when parents must stop forking over money, housing, and provision to motivate their adult children to take care of themselves.

Our church was led to have a "Basket of Abundance" one year. It was a big basket with a set of ceramic hands in the bottom of it which represented God's hands. Our people are generous and made offerings to the basket and we allowed people to take money from it to meet urgent needs like medical bills, avoid utility shutoffs, help them pay their rent, buy food, etc.

A lovely young couple with an infant child began attending our church. As we ministered to them their very first Sunday we found they were about to be evicted from their home because they didn't have the money to pay the rent. We gladly let them take from the basket of abundance to meet their need.

They continued to dip into the basket a couple of times a month for money for groceries, etc. A month later they were about to evicted again, so we let them take money for rent. It became apparent they would rather let others help pay their bills than find a job, and they depleted the Basket of Abundance.

When their next rent was due, they called and asked to meet with me, hoping for another handout. My wife and I agreed to meet with them and I explained what the Bible says about the responsibility to take care of one's own family. I asked the young man if he would take a job if I could help him find one. He said he would, and I offered to loan him the money for the current month's rent if he would go to work and pay me back by giving me 10% of each paycheck. He said yes and we drew up a contract, signed it, and we loaned them the rent money.

I called my oldest son, Eric, who is a hard working contractor, and he agreed to hire the man for a fair wage. The man did show up for work at 6:00 a.m. the next day, but failed to show for work the following day, so I called him, and he said the work was too hard. He finally paid back his loan when they got their tax return, but they continued to live off mooch. I tried to make it clear that he had a full time job already. His job was to leave every morning and go from business to business, applying for a job until he got one! I told him to find *a* job right away and quit waiting for *the* job he wanted.

They quit coming to church after their "free lunch" dried up, but he came back a few months later and said he was called to be a missionary and wondered if we would support him. I told him "absolutely not!" Jesus taught "He who is responsible in that which is least will be given more, but he who is not responsible in that which is least, even what he has will be taken away and given to another" (See Luke 16:10 for example).

This man's first responsibility was to take care of his wife and son, and until he was faithful in that, it would be a mistake to support him in ministry.

Christians should be the best, most reliable, and productive workers regardless of their career. Laziness is not a Kingdom value. When Believers work harder and with better attitudes than others, they will receive inheritance from the Lord. Believers are called to work at whatever job they have as serving the Lord.

📖 Whatever you do, work at it with all your heart, as working for the Lord, not for human masters, since you know that *you will receive an inheritance from the Lord* as a reward. *It is the Lord Christ you are serving.* Colossians 3:23-24 NIV (Italicized for emphasis).

Work is not a curse, but there is a curse against the ease of work, productivity, and prosperity which entered through Adam's fall. God cursed the ground with thorns and thistles. Adam still tended his crops but now had to till and cultivate by the sweat of his brow. He had to work harder and harder to earn less. There were thorns and thistles to contend with. To the Jewish people the thorn bush actually became a symbol for the curse of poverty.

The curse against Adam's work in Genesis 3:17-19 immediately made his work harder. He had to put forth greater effort for less increase. Evidently he began to sweat, perhaps for the first time.

It is interesting the word "sweat" is mentioned first soon after Adam sinned and God warned him, "by the sweat of your brow you will eat your food until you return to the ground." Everything grew more difficult for Adam after the curse. The last verse using the word "sweat" is really interesting because it refers to Jesus, whom the Bible refers to as the "second Adam."

📖 And being in anguish, he prayed more earnestly, and *his sweat was like drops of blood falling to the ground.* Luke 22:44 NIV (Italicized for emphasis).

Jesus expands the thought of how the curse of poverty works to spiritual poverty in the Parable of the four soils (Matthew 13, Mark 4, Luke 8). A parable is an earthly story with a heavenly meaning. Consider how Mark shares the heavenly meaning of the good seed of the Gospel which was sown among thorns.

📖 Now these are the ones sown among *thorns*; they are the ones who hear the word, and the cares of this world, the deceitfulness of riches, and the desires for other things *entering in choke the word, and **it** becomes unfruitful.* Mark 4:18-19 (Italicized and bold print for emphasis).

The word "it" in Mark 4:18 actually refers to the good word of the Gospel which is sown into humans. The Gospel seed becomes unfruitful in the lives of people caught up in the cares of this world and the deceitfulness of riches! The unfruitfulness caused by the cares of this world, the deceitfulness of riches, and desires for other things of no more value than thorns and thistles in the Kingdom of God. When we worry about money, housing, food and clothing, it shows we are trusting ourselves or others rather than the Lord. Jesus calls us to the opposite.

📖 But seek first His kingdom and His righteousness, and all these things will be added to you. Matthew 6:33 NASB.

If you read the context of Matthew 6:33, you will see it tells us to trust God with our needs, but it does not relieve us from the responsibility of doing what God tells us to do. Seeking God's Kingdom means seeking the rein of Christ in our lives, which includes receiving His imputed righteousness by faith. Righteousness also means being in the right place, at the right time, with the right people, doing the right things! Part of seeking first the Kingdom of God and his righteousness is seeking a good job where you can work, witness, and receive income to bless you, your family, and Kingdom endeavors.

There may be a curse of poverty at work when healthy people are unable to find or keep a good job. In light of the curse of poverty symbolized by thorns and thistles, it is interesting how Matthew sums up the blessing of seed sown into good Kingdom soil.

📖 But the seed falling on good soil refers to someone who hears the word and understands it. This is the one who produces a crop, yielding a hundred, sixty or thirty times what was sown." Matthew 13: 23 NIV.

Let's take this all back to the blood Jesus shed from when the thorns and thistles of Adam's curse became His mocking crown. Jesus, the Son of God, wore the crown of thorns. On behalf of sinners He allowed Himself to be stripped naked and hung on the Cross, cursed by God. I love something written in an article by Jud Davis on the Internet. He says:

"The story of the Bible is this. Adam comes naked to a live tree and spiritually murders the entire human race by a single act of disobedience. Jesus comes to a dead tree and allows Himself to be stripped naked. Then, in the ultimate act of obedience—His very death after a lifetime of full and total obedience to God—He makes alive all those who would ever by God's grace repent of their sins and trust in Him alone for salvation."[1]

Jesus totally emptied himself. He became poor for our sakes. He willingly became subject to public humiliation in order to break the power of shame off those who will follow Him. Try to visualize what Jesus went through before He ever made it to the cross. Imagine yourself as part of the crowd standing by as Jesus went through what we call "The Passion."

Picture yourself going through what Jesus did. Imagine being stripped in public, then having a king's robe forced over you. Envision having a thorny crown pushed into your skin. Picture the mocking worship and being spit upon. Visualize having a staff forced into your hand and then yanked from your hand and being beaten on the head repeatedly with it. Jesus was a bloody mess and traumatized with abuse before his hands were ever nailed to the cross.

📖 Then the governor's soldiers took Jesus into the Praetorium and gathered the whole company of soldiers around him. *They stripped him* and *put a scarlet robe on him,* and then *twisted together a crown of thorns and set it on his head.* They put a staff in his right hand. Then they knelt in front of him and mocked him. "Hail, king of the Jews!" they said. *They spit on him, and took the staff and struck him on the head again and again.* Matthew 27:27-30 NIV (Italicized for emphasis).

Jesus wore a crown of thorns; "Poverty" on His head. I've had my head poked with thorns when cutting wood or pushing through brambles. Thorn pokes are extremely painful. They turn red and hurt for days.

Jesus had a whole crown of thorns placed on His head. He broke Adam's curse of poverty, and we have a blood covenant with Him and through Him to work and make good money, to break curses of poverty and mental poverty, and to make the devil give back our money! We must apply it to enjoy it – just like salvation. Jesus died that all might be saved, but it takes an act of faith in receiving these blessings to have them.

Spirits of mental poverty plot to keep you poor through twisted mindsets concerning wealth. When people cannot get out of financial problems, regardless of how much money they make, demons of mental poverty may be at work. They short circuit your thinking about making money, spending money, giving, investing, and anything else which brings increase.

I remember a dear family in one church I pastored long before I understood how curses of poverty and spirits of mental poverty worked. They received a good sized inheritance which could have paid off all their bills, helped them make a down payment on a decent home, and increase their standard of living. But their thinking was off so the money ran through their fingers like water. Like many who win lotteries, or receive large settlements, they were in worse shape a few years later than they were before their great blessing of wealth.

The curse of poverty makes everything harder. Before God cursed the ground, Adam was blessed. God blessed his work and it yielded great abundance. But when the curse came, the ground which once yielded abundance was cursed and Adam had to work harder and harder to barely get by. I used to live like this and many still live there, existing paycheck to paycheck – and that was when I received regular paychecks rather than pay based on the willingness and ability of a small congregation to meet our church budget.

The devil wants to hold us under a curse of poverty. God wants us to be so blessed we can leave an inheritance to our grandchildren.

📖 A good man *leaves an inheritance* for his children's children, but a sinner's wealth is stored up for the righteous. Proverbs 13:22 NIV (Italicized for emphasis).

I cannot and do not believe God wants us to live as paupers and stick our children with the burden of paying for our funerals. God not only wants us to have enough for ourselves but also an inheritance to leave our children and grandchildren.

I know a wonderful couple who inherited enough money to pay cash for a house! Both the man and his sister inherited the same amount. His parents were not rich but they built a sizable inheritance to pass on. God wants to release such favor through us to our children!

Even though Jesus became poor for our sakes, He always had enough for himself and for others in need. He became poor when He left the splendor of heaven, but He always had all the food and clothing he needed. Once, when He needed money to pay taxes, God had a fish waiting with a gold coin in its mouth to take care of that bill. I jokingly say I tried that before my taxes were due, and wasn't even able to catch a fish! The point is: Jesus was never in want. Do you think He wants any of us to be in want? Doesn't He promise to supply all our needs?

The Church is called to help those who cannot help themselves, including the disabled, orphans, widows, and the disadvantaged. Still, the New Testament says those who are able to take care of their families are responsible to do so. Larry Huch wrote "that if people are able to work and are not working they are living by mooch, not by faith!"[2]

Living by faith includes working for a living, believing that God will bless your labor!

We have been redeemed from the curse of poverty by the blood of the Lamb. Jesus took the curse of thorns, shed His blood and broke that curse of poverty. Now, if we will appropriate what He has done -- we too can walk in the blessing of provision God wants to release to us, for us and even for our children.

Remember the questions I asked at the beginning of this chapter? The first one was "Do you want to be poor or prosperous?" We have a choice in the matter. Jesus shed His blood to break the curse of poverty when He wore the crown of thorns. When we apply that blood, by faith, we can break personal and ancestral curses of poverty and invoke the blessing of prosperity.

Breaking the Curse and Invoking the Blessing:

- ☩ I am redeemed by the blood of the Lamb from the hand of the enemy and from poverty.
- ☩ In Jesus' Name I apply the drops from Jesus' bleeding brow to win back my prosperity!
- ☩ I break every curse of poverty and command the spirit of mental poverty to leave me now. (Expel)
- ☩ Jesus became poor for my sake so I may be rich through Him.
- ☩ I now invoke God's blessing of riches through Christ.
- ☩ Father, help me work hard, and produce wealth to bless my family and Your Kingdom.
- ☩ Devil, give me back my money!
- ☩ In Jesus' Name, amen.

Addendum on Prosperity

I did not teach about tithing in this chapter, even though tithing is prerequisite to God rebuking the devourer (See Malachi 3:6-12). I do want to mention some things God is teaching me about sowing financial seed into good soil. Pam and I attended a conference last fall (2015) when our pay for the week was $180.00. Our hotel for the weekend was more than our paycheck. We had little extra to give and were thankful for the $1.00 menu at McDonalds.

A minister friend noticed we didn't have money to sow, and slipped some cash into our hands. I'm not sure how much he put in my hand, but it was a $20.00 bill with another bill folded inside. We put that in the offering and then during the next offering we emptied our pockets and sowed the rest of the money we had into the good soil there. We have increased our sowing since then and listen to what is happing!

A few of the blessings we've received in the next few months included:

$750.00 in unexpected and unsolicited tithes to our church from woman in California. Two "blessing tithes" to me from a woman in Kalamazoo adding up to nearly $400.00. She says she gets "unexpected financial blessings" in the tune of thousands of dollars to date, every time she does something special for me and Freedom Ministries.

The day before I finished this chapter, our church received a tithe of $500.00 with a promise of the same each month until this woman from the east side of our state finds a new church. Since we sowed the good seed, we also received a $60.00 blessing to me from a pastor in Kalamazoo. Another church in Kalamazoo began sowing $50.00 per month into Doug Carr Freedom Ministries.

Just before I sent a new syllabus to the printer I received a $250.00 tithe from a prayer ministry in Grand Rapids which paid over half of the cost of our newest syllabus. In addition to all this, a woman from our church was moved to give Pam and I a wonderful, all-expense paid, weekend at Essenhause Inn in Middlebury, Indiana which included a marvelous buffet dinner and breakfast!

We have learned you cannot out give God and He truly wants us to break every curse of poverty and walk in the blessing of abundance.

Breaking the Curse and Invoking the Blessing:

- ✝ Father, I confess and repent of withholding my full tithe from You.
- ✝ I have trusted my stinginess more than I have trusted your generosity.
- ✝ I ask You to remove every spirit of mental poverty from me and correct my mindset concerning earning, spending, and giving. (Expel)
- ✝ Please show me where and when You want me to sow seed in good soil and teach me to trust You to multiply all seed sown.
- ✝ I declare, according to Luke 6:38, that I can never out give you and with the measure I use it will be measured back to me. Amen.

Endnotes:

[1] answersingenesis.org/.../the-splendor-of-thorns by Jud Davis on May 27, 2009; last featured April 15, 2012.

[2] Larry Huch, The 7 Places Jesus Shed His Blood. Whitaker House, 2000, 2004, page 60.

TAKING BACK SUCCESS THROUGH HIS HANDS
From Disappointment to Divine Appointment!

Take a look at your hands? Do you have blessed hands or cursed hands? Have your hands prospered and brought blessings to you or others -- or have they been used of the enemy to kill, steal, and destroy?

Regardless of how your hands have been used in the past – they can be blessed from here on. Last night was my turn to preach at the Branch County Jail. I wanted to preach on taking back success through the blood from Jesus' hands. After a song, Chaplain Carl shared a Scripture, took prayer requests, and prayed before I preached. He told us to turn to Philippians 4 and I saw a note I had put in my "preaching Bible" and forgotten. That note changed the whole mood of my message:

When you focus on Jesus' scars, it leads to victory.
When you focus on your own scars, it leads to defeat.

Many of the dear men sitting in that jail service were there because of things they did with their hands! Whether using or manufacturing drugs, stealing, some form of physical abuse or excessive drinking -- their hands had brought curse rather than blessing. If they -- if we obsess over the wrong things we have done with our hands, it will lead to defeat. If we look at the scars on Jesus' hands, however, and apply the blood from His hands, we will enter victory!

When the first Adam was created, he ruled with his hands. Everything he put his hands to prospered. He was able to take dominion and subdue the earth, but when he stretched out his hand and took the forbidden fruit, his blessed hands were cursed. Unfortunately, his curse and iniquity passed down to his own children and the entire human race. The wages of sin soon brought death as Adam's oldest son murdered his younger brother. People began failing for the first time. Projects were started but not finished. Idle hands became the devil's workshop.

Thankfully, Jesus' blood can reverse that curse! Jesus' hands were pierced to break the curse against the work of our hands in order to bring us into fullness.

Human hands can be a marvelous blessing or a horrible curse to us and to others. Do you struggle with disappointment? Most people have since sin brought a curse against the work of our hands. God truly wants to break the "dis" off His "appointment" for our lives and the work of our hands.

Jesus, the second Adam, redeemed back for us the power to use our hands to bless rather than to hurt, and to prosper through the work of our hands, if only we will apply the blood of His bleeding hands to break every curse against the work of our hands.

Human hands can be marvelous. I love watching my wife's hands as she plays the piano. It is fascinating to watch the hands of people while they are worshipping on their instruments. The connection between heart, brain, and hands in producing music is awesome as it draws you to the heart of God! Watching the hands of an artist, a carpenter, a mechanic, or a mother with her baby is amazing.

Human hands can be cruel and horrible. I once sat at a table with a young girl. Every time her father moved his hands to take a bite of food, she flinched. God created hands to minister love, to create and produce wealth, for prayer and praise, and to do the works of Jesus. The devil wants to use them to kill, steal, and destroy. There are over 2,100 Bible verses with the word "hand" or "hands." There is a great contrast between "blessed hands and "cursed hands." Consider the work of your own hands as you look at this comparative list of blessed hands versus cursed hands:

BLESSED HANDS	CURSED HANDS
Are comforting	Are traumatizing
Protect others	Murderous
May be guided by angels	Idolatrous
Innocent	Deceptive
May help others	May harm others
Responsible	Irresponsible
Guided by God	Control by anger
Spread out to release miracles	Destructive
Prepare acceptable sacrifice	Unacceptable offerings
Sanctified by blood	Unclean

Bless others	Curse others
Release anointing	Entrap people
Set people/things apart for God	The devil's workshop
Bear good testimony	Release fear
Rejoice in the Lord	Wring in despair
Blessed of the Lord unto good works	Cursed
Productive for good.	Cause trouble
All the works of blessed by the Lord.	Evil recompense
Please the Lord	Provoke the Lord
Strengthened for victory	Victimized
Diligent	Lazy
Lifted to the Lord	Lifted to self
Holy hands	Unholy
Laying on to release Holy Spirit	Spoil others
Laying to release spiritual gifts.	Take from others.

Are your hands blessed or cursed? Consider the following:

📖 But his bow remained in strength, And the arms of *his hands were made strong* by the hands of the Mighty God of Jacob (From there is the Shepherd, the Stone of Israel), Genesis 49:24 (Italicized for emphasis).

📖 "For *the Lord your God has blessed you in all the work of your hand*. He knows your trudging through this great wilderness. These forty years the Lord your God has been with you; you have lacked nothing." Deuteronomy 2:7 (Italicized for emphasis).

📖 You shall surely give to him, and your heart should not be grieved when you give to him, because for this thing *the Lord your God will bless you in all your works and in all to which you put your hand*. Deuteronomy 15:10 (Italicized for emphasis).

📖 The Lord will open to you His good treasure, the heavens, to give the rain to your land in its season, and *to bless all the work of your hand*. You shall lend to many nations, but you shall not borrow. Deuteronomy 28:12.

📖 "The Lord rewarded me according to my righteousness; *According to the cleanness of my hands He has recompensed me*. 2 Samuel 22:21 (Italicized for emphasis).

📖 *He teaches my hands to make war,* so that my arms can bend a bow of bronze. 2 Samuel 22:35 (Italicized for emphasis).

📖 But you, be strong and *do not let your hands be weak,* for your work shall be rewarded!" 2 Chronicles 15:7 (Italicized for emphasis).

📖 And I told them of the hand of my God which had been good upon me, and also of the king's words that he had spoken to me. So they said, "Let us rise up and build." *Then they set their hands to this good work* . . . For they all were trying to make us afraid, saying, *"Their hands will be weakened in the work,* and it will not be done." Now therefore, O God, strengthen my hands. Nehemiah 2:18, 6:9 (Italicized for emphasis).

📖 And let the beauty of the Lord our God be upon us, *and establish the work of our hands for us; Yes, establish the work of our hands.* Psalm 90:17 (Italicized for emphasis).

📖 How long will you slumber, O sluggard? When will you rise from your sleep? A little sleep, a little slumber, *a little folding of the hands to sleep*—so shall your poverty come on you like a prowler, and your need like an armed man. Proverbs 6:9-11.

📖 And *through the hands of the apostles* many signs and wonders were done among the people. And they were all with one accord in Solomon's Porch. Acts 5:12 (Italicized for emphasis).

📖 Draw near to God and He will draw near to you. *Cleanse your hands, you sinners; and purify your hearts, you double-minded.* James 4:8 (Italicized for emphasis).

Considering these verses, do you believe your hands are blessed, cursed, or somewhere in between? Jesus' bleeding hands win back dominion over what we touch! When God created Adam and Eve he gave them dominion over everything on the earth. Consider God's original prototype for men and women.

📖 Then God said, "Let Us make man in Our image, according to Our likeness; *let them have dominion* over the fish of the sea, over the birds of the air, and over the cattle, over all the earth and over every creeping thing that creeps on the earth." So God created man in His own image; in the image of God He created him; male and female He created them. Then God blessed them, and God said to them, "Be fruitful and multiply; fill the earth and subdue it; *have dominion* over the fish of the sea, over the birds of the air, and over every living thing that moves on the earth." Genesis 1:26-28 (Italicized for emphasis.)

For centuries the Church has understood what mankind lost in the fall. Unfortunately, we haven't understood how Jesus redeemed *everything* lost in the fall and wants to restore us so we can bring transformation to the world. The whole earth is desperately waiting for the true children of God to manifest His rule again.

📖 For the earnest expectation of *the creation eagerly waits for the revealing of the sons of God*. For the creation was subjected to futility, not willingly, but because of Him who subjected it in hope; because the creation itself also will be delivered from the bondage of corruption into the glorious liberty of the children of God. For we know that the whole creation groans and labors with birth pangs together until now. Not only that, but we also who have the firstfruits of the Spirit, even we ourselves groan within ourselves, eagerly waiting for the adoption, the redemption of our body. Romans 8:19-23 (Italicized for emphasis).

The fullness of the sons of God will not be completed until Jesus returns as conquering King, but we certainly are called to live and rule as the children of God.

In the parable about the minas Jesus mentioned the landowner told his tenants to "occupy until I come" (Luke 19:13). This parable shows the Lord does not want us to hand the whole world over to the devil in a handbasket. Now we, the children of God, are called to forcibly advance His Kingdom on this earth (Matthew 11:12).

📖 From the days of John the Baptist until now the kingdom of heaven suffers violent assault, and violent men seize it by force [as a precious prize]. Matthew 11:12 AMP.

Jesus took back everything Adam lost through the fall, by redeeming it for us through His blood! Psalm 68:18 implies Jesus *received gifts from* men. Ephesians 4:8 says Jesus *gave gifts* to men.

Somewhere between Jesus' crucifixion and ascension, Jesus took back the dominion and authority humans forfeited through sin, so He might restore it to His Apostolic Church!   I will share more on this later.

Adam was cursed and his ground was cursed but Jesus bought the blessing back for us and gives us opportunity to take it back for ourselves through His blood.

The life of the Patriarch Joseph demonstrates how God can and will bless the work of those who will truly serve God through their work.

📖 And his master saw that the Lord was with him and that *the Lord made all he did to prosper in his hand.* Genesis 39:3 (Italicized for emphasis).

If God so blessed the work of Joseph's hands after God cursed the ground in Adam's day, and after He covered the earth with water during Noah's day, can He not bless the work of our hands in our day?

Before Jesus' hands were nailed to the cross, He used them to heal the sick, multiply the loaves and fishes, raise the dead to life, comfort the grieving, and bless the children.

On the cross, Jesus' hands were left powerless. He could barely pull Himself up to gasp a breath of air because of the pain of pulling against His pierced hands.

When those spikes were driven into Jesus' hands and His blood spilled from them, He broke the curse against the work of our hands and bought back our dominion and authority so we rule in and for the Kingdom.

Jesus' hands bled, therefore we can lay hands on the sick and they will be healed.

There are times when my hands feel like they are burning with anointing to heal and deliver, and we have a fourteen-year old Granddaughter whose hands begin to burn with anointing when she is to lay her hands on the sick. We can lift up our hands and tell demons to flee. (Keep your faith focused on the Lord, not the heat in your hands!)

Jesus' hands bled, we can lay hands on the empty and they will be filled. We can raise holy hands in prayer and see great things happen.

At one time our small city had a house of prostitution. It went under the guise of a health spa and massage center. Chief Ally, our then Police Chief, told the Minister's Association he wasn't able to do anything about it. He knew what was going on there and even said the only Health issue there was the STD's people carried after they visited the spa. But he couldn't find a credible witness of what went on there, though he had plenty of volunteers. So my prayer partner, some Kingdom-minded pastors, and I prayed around that building the police couldn't shut down. Within weeks it was closed. We've had similar success with a couple of bars known for their perversity.

Because of what Jesus did -- we can take back our authority and rule with our hands. Think of the power a 190 pound policeman has to stop an 80,000 pound 18-wheeler. He can do so because of the authority invested in him.

Jesus delegated His authority and power to us! Once I took a giant of a man through deliverance. He probably outweighed me by 150 pounds, and the demon in him stirred him to jump out of his chair so hard it shattered into pieces. He instantly stood in front of me and I think his demon wanted to kill me, but I raised my hand and quietly but firmly said "Stop it!" I then pulled up a steel chair told him to sit down. He complied but ripped his long-sleeved church off, began flexing his muscles, and singing "Jesus loves me" in a mocking voice. I cast the demon out of him and he began weeping repentantly. How could I do that? By using the authority Jesus redeemed back for me through His bleeding hands.

Jesus' hands bled to break the curse against our creativity and productivity. We have to intentionally apply His blood to break the curse against the work of our hands.

His precious blood releases a blessing over the work of our hands so we too may work miracles, multiply wealth, meet personal needs and bless others with need. It is impossible to please God without faith, however. We must purposely invoke God's blessing over our hands and work.

Breaking the Curse and Invoking the Blessing:

✝ In Jesus' Name I apply the drops from Jesus' Bleeding Hands and take back dominion over everything I touch and attempt with my hands.

✝ I break the power of every curse against the work of my hands, or the ability to use my hands to create wealth, and bless others.

✝ I break every curse against my creativity and productivity.

✝ I declare my hands are redeemed by the blood of the Lamb out of the hand of the enemy!

✝ I cast out every demon working against my authority to use my hands for God's purposes. (Expel)

✝ I invoke Abba Father's blessing over my hands so I can bless my family, my church, and the world.

✝ I invoke Jesus' blessing over everything I lay my hands to.

✝ Father, make my hands creative and productive for You and Your Kingdom.

✝ In Jesus' Name and through the blood from His nail pierced hands. Amen.

TAKING BACK DOMINION THROUGH HIS FEET
From Victimized to Victorious!

Have you ever noticed how some people can speak quietly and people follow their directions, while others yell and scream and no one pays attention? In some homes one parent has obedient children and the other has disobedient children, and they are the same children!

Jesus said "All authority in heaven and on earth has been given to me, therefore go and make disciples of all nations" (From Matthew 18:18-19). Jesus wants us to forcefully advance His Kingdom through the authority He has delegated to us. So why are there some Christians who can't even take authority over a headache? It is a matter of breaking the curse against one's authority and taking back the authority Jesus redeemed for us.

Adam lost his dominion and authority in the garden through sin. He could no longer keep weeds and thistles at bay or even keep his oldest son from murdering his second son. God wants His people to be the head and not the tail, but that level of dominion only comes with the level of authority only made possible through application of the blood of Jesus! Since Jesus bought back for us the authority Adam lost, isn't it time we learn to walk in it?

We are to use His delegated authority to win the lost, equip the saved, and make true disciples, but it doesn't stop there. Rather than let the world mold us into its systems, we are to forcibly advance the Kingdom in every segment of society including: families, government, religion, business, education, arts and entertainment and media.

We are to carry His authority into places where we work and shop and play to impact all those places with Kingdom life and values. Church is good, but Jesus preached the Kingdom! He told us to use the authority granted to us to advance His Kingdom on earth. Early in His ministry Jesus taught it will take forceful men and women to lay hold of the dominion and rule of the Kingdom of Heaven.

📖 From the days of John the Baptist until now, the kingdom of heaven has been forcefully advancing, and *forceful men lay hold of it*. Matthew 11:12 NIV (Italicized for emphasis).

In the Old Testament, Kings would be deposed by putting your feet on their necks (Joshua 10:24). Better than a knockout in boxing, victorious Kings would have their soldiers put their feet on the necks of defeated kings. Bill Hamon had a dream about this and told about it in the article to the Elijah list on November 13, 2007. *"IT'S TIME to PUT OUR FEET on the NECK of the ENEMY."* He exposed five enemies whose necks we need to put our feet on. Let me quote from his article.

Five Spirits Being Exposed

We knew the Lord was telling us that we have victory over these five "kings" (demonic spirits) that have been coming against us. Jane Hamon helped research the meaning of each of the king's names to understand the spiritual implications for the Body of Christ today. As you read these brief descriptions of each of them, consider how these spirits may have had access to your life: Adoni-Zedek, king of Jerusalem (this is before the Israelites took possession), represents a spirit of oppression that leads to injustice, fear, poverty, confusion and defeat. This spirit is after your peace and tries to instill worry and fear. The oppression can cause head pain and constriction in the chest.

Hoham, king of Hebron, represents the spirit of religion, which drives people into religious performance to try to perfect themselves through legalism rather than the leading of the Holy Spirit. This can lead to passivity, retreat, moral corruption, exhaustion, weariness and broken relationships. It causes an inability to move forward in the things of God and will always resist spiritual warfare.

Piram, king of Jarmuth, represents a spirit of besiegement that can lead to barrenness, poverty, isolation and death. It wants to keep you wild, unbridled and too proud to submit to true spiritual authority so that you will be isolated.

Japhia, king of Lachish, represents a spirit of blindness. This spirit will try to get you to shine the light on yourself and demand your rights, so that you take God's glory for yourself and lose the ability to receive revelation from God. It can darken your spiritual understanding, bringing a lack of joy and a feeling of bondage.

Debir, king of Eglon, represents a spirit of accusation. It seeks to get you to attack others' reputations, to bring discredit to leaders, and to stop true prophetic revelation from going forth or to release false prophets. Its goal is to cut off the voice of the Lord, stop the war cry of the saints and remove the presence of God from your midst.

After Joshua and the Israelites defeated the Amorite armies, Joshua had the five kings removed from the cave. Joshua asked his military captains to put their feet on the necks of the five kings. This is what the Holy Spirit is saying to each of us: "I have given you the victory over these spirits that have come against you and tried to bring you into a place of decrease. It's time to put your feet on the neck of the enemy and enforce your victory!"

I appreciate Bill and Jane Hamon's encouragement for Believer's to exercise authority against the powers of darkness. God promised Joshua could take possession of the land everywhere he walked in authority.

📖 Every place on which the sole of your foot treads shall be yours: Deuteronomy. 10:24a.

The word translated "set" in the NIV or "tread" in the KJV is the Hebrew word "darak." It is a word that denotes great authority. It isn't merely taking a walk, but putting your foot down. It means forcibly advancing the kingdom. It is the same word that is used in Hebrew armies. When the Sergeant cries out "darak," soldiers mount their weapons for war.

When we prayer walk our neighborhoods we are putting this principle to practice. We pray against the things that bring darkness and pray for the things which spread the light of the Kingdom.

If we are going to break curses and invoke blessings we need to use the blood Jesus shed from His feet to break every curse against our dominion and invoke His Kingdom blessing and authority.

One year while I was studying apostolic church government, I came across what appeared to be a contradiction in Scripture. I mentioned this in the last chapter but want to cover it more thoroughly here. I was studying Ephesians 4 and followed the cross reference to Psalm 68.

Psalm 68:18 to Ephesians 4:8 both speak of God dwelling on earth with one notable difference.

📖 This is why it says: "When he ascended on high, he took many captives *and gave gifts to his people."* Ephesians 4:8 NIV (Italicized for emphasis).

📖 When you ascended on high, you took many captives; *you received gifts from people,* even from the rebellious--that you, Lord God, might dwell *there.* Psalm 68:18 NIV. (Italicized for emphasis)

What really caught my attention is the use of the word *"received"* in Psalm 68 and having it replaced with the word *"gave"* in Ephesians 4. Since Holy Spirit inspired those who wrote the Scripture, I asked Him why He used "received" in the Psalm and "gave" in Ephesians. Here is what I sensed Jesus saying.

> *I paid the total price for the sin of the world on the Cross. I spent eternity in hell over the next three days. While there I took back the authority and dominion Satan usurped through man's rebellion. I said, "give it back!" Then when I ascended I established apostolic government for My Church and gave back to Kingdom people the gifts of Kingdom authority and dominion I redeemed for them.*

Psalm 68 refers to when Jesus died, and I believe, visited hell. Jesus took back the dominion and authority the devil usurped through rebellious people. He took back the dominion Adam and Eve lost. He redeemed the dominion Saul forsook. Jesus so completely bought back the human authority and dominion mankind lost that He could release the Great Commission along with the authority to fulfil it!

When Jesus ascended into heaven, He took those mantles of dominion and authority He redeemed with blood, and restored them to Kingdom people through apostolic kingdom authority. Now He says "All authority has been given unto me, therefore go!" (Matthew 28:18-19) Let me show you the extent in which Jesus wants us to operate in His authority.

📖 "Most assuredly, I say to you, he who believes in Me, the works that I do he will do also; and greater works than these he will do, because I go to My Father. And whatever you ask in My name, that I will do, that the Father may be glorified in the Son. If you ask anything in My name, I will do it. John 14:12-14.

Jesus bought back for us the authority Adam lost! We can apply this concept to winning our children back to the Lord, prayer-walking around our schools or community, or whatever. Jesus won back our authority to take dominion. (Prayer-walking is simply walking and praying over things we see or sense as we are walking past homes, schools, neighborhoods, and the like.)

We are not little baby Christians who have accepted little baby Jesus into our little baby hearts. We are men and women of God who have the authority to take back our families, schools, cities, government, and country for the King of Kings!

Most translations of Psalm 8:5 have a glaring mistake based, I believe, on the devil's attempt to keep us from realizing we can walk in restored dominion and authority because of what Jesus did. It seems far too easy to throw up our hands thinking we can't do anything about the mess the world is in, so why try? Let me share Psalm 8:5 from the New King James Version along with its footnote.

📖 For You have made him *a little lower than the angels*, and You have crowned him with glory and honor. Psalm 8:5 (Italicized for emphasis).

Most reliable translations include a footnote stating the word translated "angels" is "Elohim" which most scholars recognize as a name for God. Notice the footnote from the New King James Version. "Psalm 8:5 Hebrew Elohim, God; Septuagint, Syriac, Targum, and Jewish tradition translate as angels."

You may wonder what difference it makes whether Elohim is properly translated "God" rather than "angels." It has to do with dominion and authority. Humans, before the fall and after Christ's ascension are a little lower than God. They are not lower than angels, especially fallen angels!

When we properly understand Jesus redeemed our dominion and authority through His blood, we will have greater confidence taking authority over the devil and all his works. Confidence, for Believers, is really faith in God!

Even though Hebrews 2 refers to Psalm 8:5 and also speaks of man being created a little lower than angels, it qualifies it by saying God has put everything under redeemed man's rule and authority.

I find it humorous how the writer couldn't remember the reference, saying "but there is a place somewhere . . ." Look at how he addresses the great authority God has given to people.

📖 But there is a place where someone has testified: "What is man that you are mindful of him, the son of man that you care for him? *You made him a little lower than the angels*; (*you* crowned him with glory and honor and *put everything under his feet*." In putting everything under him, God left nothing that is not subject to him. Yet at present we do not see everything subject to him. Hebrews 2:6-8 NIV (Italicized for emphasis).

I kept a Frank and Ernest cartoon posted in my office until it became so tattered and yellow I tossed it. Frank was lamenting about all the problems of the world and said he was tempted to ask God why He doesn't do something about them. Ernest asked, "Well, why don't you ask?" And Frank said "because I'm afraid He might ask me the same question."

God *is* asking us why we don't use the dominion and authority Jesus bought back for us. Why don't we manifest as the children of God and make this world a better place?

Why should Christians walk around like wimps? Don't we have dominion? Why should Believers give in to depression, addictions, temptation, bitterness, or defeat? Why should Christians pass by people who obviously need a touch from God? Don't we have dominion over such things?

I was totally amazed by God the first time He told me to heal a person. Even though I knew Jesus told His disciples to go forth and "heal the sick," I never dreamed I was given authority to do anything more than pray for the sick. I was in the middle of asking God to heal a man and heard Him say, "No, you heal him." I argued over this in my spirit for a while but finally relented and said "be healed in Jesus' Name." I'm not sure who was more surprised, the one healed or the one praying. I am learning Jesus meant it when He said we will do even greater things than He did if we only believe. So do we have dominion or not?

A similar thing happened with casting out demons. I wasn't sure I even believed in deliverance at the time, but kept hearing the Holy Spirit tell me to cast a spirit of gambling out a woman whose life was being destroyed by her addiction to gambling. I finally gave in to casting that demon out and the woman was amazingly set free! Do we really have dominion through Jesus blood?

A neighborhood dog used to bark when I tried to write sermons or minister deliverance. I was never successful shutting it up when studying, but time and again during deliverance I would speak "be quiet in Jesus' Name" and the dog quit barking. I knew it couldn't hear my quiet command, but I exercised God-given dominion and it worked. Why don't we walk with dominion and authority?

Once while visiting an inmate in jail we were greatly disturbed by a loud and evidently demonized man who was being booked. Even though I was visiting within a somewhat soundproofed room, and the man making the disturbance was at least 70 feet away, the disturbance stopped immediately when I whispered "stop it in Jesus' name." The demons believe in a Believer's dominion and authority, why don't we?

There have been a few times when God has allowed me to use dominion over weather. The first was just before a church picnic started. We continued our plans even though the forecast was stormy. I watched as the wind picked up, storm clouds gathered, and we heard thunder. I raised my hands and spoke to the weather and commanded the storm to dissipate. It did, and the rain didn't come back until the party was over and the last guest had gone home.

One summer we were scheduled to build a pole barn. By the time the permits were finalized, my oldest son only had one week left when he could build the barn with a little help from me. Unfortunately, it was mid-June and the weather forecast was for thunderstorms every day that week. Every time it started to thunder or rain, however, I lifted my hands to the clouds and commanded them not to rain. It rained and stormed hard several times that week, but never when we working!

I'm quick to admit praying this has seldom worked for me when I wanted to go fishing, but every time I've sensed Holy Spirit's leading to make such declaration it has worked.

Think of Jesus' feet. They walked on water! They carried Him everywhere God wanted Him to go. Jesus certainly had power to tread upon the lion and the cobra and to trample the great lion and the dragon (Psalm 91:13). Jesus could walk on water, move through a crowd undetected, stand up to the very men who were trying to kill Him, turn over the tables of the money-changers and keep on keeping on regardless of what came against Him.

His final steps before the resurrection, however, were to Golgotha where His hands and feet were nailed to the cross. He had been beaten beyond recognition. When His feet were nailed to the cross they didn't retain enough strength to hold Him up to where He could catch His breath. For a few hours on that cruel cross Jesus came under Adam's curse and lost His dominion and authority. The blood from His precious feet broke that curse against man's dominion and redeemed for us the power to walk in Jesus' delegated dominion and authority. Wow, God!

Now if we will apply the blood of Jesus bleeding feet, we can break the curse against our dominion and authority. If we invoke Jesus blessing of "As the Father has sent me, so send I you," we will walk in His dominion and authority as we advance His Kingdom on earth (See John 20:21).

Breaking the Curse and Invoking the Blessing:

✝ In Jesus' powerful Name I apply the drops from Jesus' Bleeding Feet to regain the rule wherever I tread!

✝ I declare my authority and dominion are redeemed by the blood of the Lamb out of the hand of the enemy!

✝ I break every curse against my dominion and authority; first over my own life and sin, and then over where I live, walk, and work.

✝ In Jesus' name I cast out every demon working against my authority and dominion as a Believer. (Expel)

✝ Father, by faith in what Jesus' did when He shed His blood for me, I invoke Your blessing of power, dominion, and authority to advance your Kingdom forcibly where I live and work.

✝ I take back by faith, everything Jesus restored to His people through His blood.

✝ I take back authority over sin, disease, demons, and even weather as you lead me.

✝ I invoke Your blessing to walk in the authority of Christ and take Kingdom dominion.

✝ In Jesus' Name, amen.

TAKING BACK WHOLENESS THROUGH HIS HEART
From Brokenness to Wholeness!

The first Adam's rebellion brought brokenness and fragmentation to the human race. Imagine how Adam and Eve's hearts were broken when their firstborn murdered their second son. The second Adam, Christ, was anointed to bind up the wounds of the broken-hearted.

We have studied six of the seven places where Jesus shed His blood to break seven core curses and release seven key blessings. There is Jesus' blood than meets the eye. As we look at the seventh place where Jesus shed His blood, consider the following passages: one which records Jesus' death, and two others which predict the precise manner of His death. First we look at John's words.

📖 These things happened so that the scripture would be fulfilled: "*Not one of his bones will be broken*," and, as another scripture says, "They will look on the one they have pierced." John 19:36-37 NIV (Italicized for emphasis).

In Exodus 12, God instituted Passover, telling the people to slay a perfect Lamb and take the blood of the Lamb and apply it to the sides and top of their doorframes, in the sign of a cross. The Passover was given to protect the firstborn of God's people and their flocks from being killed by the plague of death of the firstborn. When God saw the blood, He passed over and the plague did not touch them. John 19:36 refers to the unbroken bones of the Passover Lamb.

📖 In one house it shall be eaten; you shall not carry any of the flesh outside the house, *nor shall you break one of its bones*. Exodus 12:46 (Italicized for emphasis).

John 19:37, which you read earlier, refers to a prophecy in Zechariah.

📖 "And I will pour out on the house of David and the inhabitants of Jerusalem a spirit of grace and supplication. *They will look on me, the one they have pierced,* and they will mourn for him as one mourns for an only child, and grieve bitterly for him as one grieves for a firstborn son. Zechariah 12:10 NIV (Italicized for emphasis).

A great crowd surrounded Jesus as He breathed His last. They watched as soldiers thrust a spear into Jesus' side and the flow of blood and water gushed out. Very few in that crowd understood the depth of meaning in what happened right then and there.

If you have been around the Church very long, you have probably sung "Rock of Ages." The first verse says, "*Rock of ages, cleft for me; Let me hide myself in Thee; Let the water and the blood, From thy wounded side which flowed, Be of sin the double cure, Save from wrath and make me pure.*"[1]

I wonder how often we have sung this hymn without understanding the words. I trust they will mean more to us from now on. The lyrics from another song came to me from my youth. I didn't hear this one in church. It is the Beatles song I remember as "All The Lonely People." The lyrics that played in in my spirit were: "all the lonely people, where do they all come from?" (From Eleonore Rigby.)[2]

As a minister of deep inner healing and deliverance I meet many people who are so broken hearted from past abuse they have trouble relating to their fragmented parts and find it nearly impossible to relate well to God or others. When young children are sexually abused or repeatedly beaten physically or emotionally they cannot handle the trauma. When the trauma is severe, parts of them actually break off and go into hiding somewhere within their psyche.

This makes it so they can't even relate to all their own inner parts, let alone relate to others or God. Most people have some fragmentation, but some are so broken they have Dissociative Identity Disorder (D.I.D.).

Let me share the introduction from an excellent WebMD article about D.I.D.:

> Dissociative identity disorder (previously known as multiple personality disorder) is thought to be an effect of severe trauma during early childhood, usually extreme, repetitive physical, sexual, or emotional abuse.
>
> What Is Dissociative Identity Disorder?

Most of us have experienced mild dissociation, which is like daydreaming or getting lost in the moment while working on a project. However, dissociative identity disorder is a severe form of dissociation, a mental process which produces a lack of connection in a person's thoughts, memories, feelings, actions, or sense of identity. Dissociative identity disorder is thought to stem from trauma experienced by the person with the disorder. The dissociative aspect is thought to be a coping mechanism -- the person literally dissociates himself from a situation or experience that's too violent, traumatic, or painful to assimilate with his conscious self.[3]

So, you might ask, where is this found in the Bible? While there are several verses which speak of broken heartedness, James speaks of such fragmentation, using a compound word he may have invented: "double-minded." James says a double-minded man is unstable in all his ways.

The Greek word translated "double-minded," is only found in James 1:8 and 4:8 is "dipsuchos" and comes from two Greek words translated "two" and "soul." A double-minded person is one who has two or more breaks or fragments in their soul. They are hurt so deeply, their soul has fragmented and makes them "unstable in all their ways."

I realize "double-minded" may refer to people who are trying to walk in the world and in the Kingdom at the same time, thinking they can have the best of both worlds. At the same time, I personally believe it may also refer to people who are truly committed to the Kingdom but so broken they keep losing their way.

Many lonely people we work with have been terribly broken by pain, abuse, and trauma. Psalm 68:6 mentions God's desire to set the lonely in families. We have a mandate to reach out to lonely people and set them in our church family where they can find healing for their broken and/or lonely hearts. Jesus' heart was broken, His blood and water flowed out from His side to break the curse of brokenness and release the blessing of wholeness.

Jesus had already given up his spirit when the executioners came by to break the legs of the three men hanging on crosses. Since Jesus had already died they didn't break his legs but one did thrust a spear into his side and out flowed blood and water. That burst of blood and water has more significance than most people notice. It was a vital part of Jesus's mission to bind up the wounds of the brokenhearted. His heart was broken to make our hearts whole again!

📖 But one of the soldiers pierced His side with a spear, and immediately *blood and water* came out. John 19:34 (Italicized for emphasis).

It is amazing how Scripture was fulfilled when the soldiers pieced Jesus' side.

We will look at the significance of the blood and water soon, but first look at how central healing broken hearts is in Jesus' ministry. In His inauguration to public ministry He quoted Isiah 61. His words are recorded by Luke.

📖 "The Spirit of the Lord is upon Me, Because He has anointed Me to preach the gospel to the poor; *He has sent Me to heal the brokenhearted*, to proclaim liberty to the captives and recovery of sight to the blind, to set at liberty those who are oppressed; to proclaim the acceptable year of the Lord." Luke 4:18-19 (Italicized for emphasis).

Central to Jesus' mission is healing the brokenhearted. Unfortunately, several English translations of the Bible overlook the Greek word "suntribo" which is translated "broken-hearted" here and in the King James Bible. It means to be "broken to shivers or broken hearted." It can refer to people being broken down personally, or to putting Satan under our feet and breaking him to shivers!

Suntribo is built on two words: "sun" which means "beside or accompany" and "tribos" (treebos) which means a worn path. I testify Jesus is still in the business of healing broken and fragmented hearts, regardless of how long they have been on that worn path!

I spent hours researching why blood and water flowed from Jesus' side when he was pierced with a spear in him to make sure He was dead. I found several scriptural reasons plus medical explanations why both blood and water flowed from His heart. Rather than using a lot of deep and detailed explanations let me summarize what I gleaned by sharing what I already sensed from Holy Spirit. Jesus died of a broken heart!

Jesus, God incarnate in human flesh, had walked with His Father from eternity. He and the Father were one, and nothing could break their oneness until Jesus became sin for us and took our sin upon Himself on the cross. One of Jesus saddest declarations came just before He gave up His spirit. I made reference of this before, but want to go a little deeper with it here.

Jesus always called God "Father," always, that is, except when His Father abandoned Him. Jesus truly took our sin upon Himself on the cross and His Heavenly Father turned away from Him because of that sin. Just before Jesus died, he used one of the most generic terms there is for God. Look at it in Matthew's Gospel.

📖 Now from the sixth hour until the ninth hour there was darkness over all the land. And about the ninth hour Jesus cried out with a loud voice, saying, "*Eli, Eli*, lama sabachthani?" that is, "*My God, My God*, why have You forsaken Me?" And Jesus cried out again with a loud voice, and yielded up His spirit. Matthew 27:45-46, 50 (Italicized for emphasis).

Jesus, who knew no sin, became sin on our behalf that we might become the righteousness of God through His shed blood. Jesus literally could not personally approach God the Father when He took our sin upon Himself. The Father looked away from Jesus' reproach and this broke Jesus' heart. He had always been with the Father, so much so He said, "If you have seen the Father, you have seen Me." On this sad day, however, Jesus cried out with a loud voice, just like others have when they had fatal heart attacks. His heart was literally broken when the full weight of our sin completely separated Him from Father God. He was so broken His heart fragmented. At that moment Jesus couldn't call God "Father." Instead He used the generic term for God, "Eli or Elohim -- God."

All four Gospels record the crucifixion of Jesus. To see the whole picture, it is good to study Matthew 26:31-27:56; Mark 14:32-15:47; Luke 22:39-49; and John 18:1-19:47. For our purpose here, I am repeating Matthew 27:45-46, 50 and adding other verses from Matthew and Luke so you can see them together.

📖 Now from the sixth hour until the ninth hour there was darkness over all the land. And about the ninth hour Jesus cried out with a loud voice, saying, "Eli, Eli, lama sabachthani?" that is, "*My God, My God, why have You forsaken Me?*" Matthew 27: 45-46 (Italicized for emphasis).

📖 And when Jesus had cried out with a loud voice, He said, "*Father, 'into Your hands I commit My spirit.*'" Having said this, He breathed His last. Luke 23:46 (Italicized for emphasis).

We should never overlook the other amazing and marvelous things which happened as Jesus died on the cross. Even the Centurion and those with him who had taken part in Jesus' crucifixion, had a change of mind when they saw what happened (Matthew 27:51-54). Look at it for yourself.

📖 Then, behold, the veil of the temple was torn in two from top to bottom; and the earth quaked, and the rocks were split, and the graves were opened; and many bodies of the saints who had fallen asleep were raised; and coming out of the graves after His resurrection, they went into the holy city and appeared to many. Matthew 27:51-53.

Jesus cried out "My God, My God, why have you forsaken me." The strongest indicator of having a broken or fragmented heart may be the burdensome weight of feeling totally forsaken by others and God, just like Jesus was. How can people return to God after feeling totally forsaken?

Amazingly, Jesus's final words on the cross, gasped after His heart literally burst were "Father, into your hands I commit My Spirit." Even when Jesus couldn't feel God or find Him, by faith He cried out "Father!" Isn't that incredible? Jesus' faith in the midst of such awful pain and betrayal opened the way for the broken-hearted to believe again! Paul wrote "Everyone who calls upon the Name of the Lord shall be saved" (Romans 10:13).

Years ago Pam and I were talking with Pastor Jack Eitelbuss. Pastor Jack was bemoaning the fact that Christians seldom use the name "Jesus" in their conversations. Even in prayer they usually refer to God using the generic term "god," rather than "Father," or "Jesus." Pam commented, "Maybe it's because they don't know Him well enough to call Him by name.

That is not what happened, however, when Jesus did not use the Father's personal name when addressing Him from the cross. He was separated from the Father as He carried our sin upon the tree. Even when Jesus didn't feel God and couldn't find Him, He still called out in faith, "Father." Shortly after this, the soldiers were commanded to break the legs of the three men hanging on their crosses. When they came to Jesus, He was already dead, so they didn't break His legs. Instead one of the soldiers pierced His heart with a sword and out poured blood and water.

Some say the blood and water which poured from Jesus' heart give medical evidence His heart was literally ruptured, but we don't need medical evidence to prove Jesus' heart was broken. Jesus experienced continual heartbreak. The crowds took advantage of His blessings, but did not follow in faith. He asked His best friends to stay awake with Him during His time of greatest trial and each one fell asleep. His disciples promised to be faithful but one denied Him, another betrayed Him, and most forsook Him when He needed them most. The crowds cried out for Barabbas to be released and Jesus to crucified. He came to His own, but His own did not receive Him. He saw the pain in His mother's eyes as He hung on a cross.

When you consider how Jesus was betrayed, falsely accused, targeted by the religious leaders, wronged by friends and enemies, scourged, crowned with thorns, forced to carry His own cross, stripped naked, and nailed hands and feet to a cross, you can easily assume His precious heart broke.

At the point of dying from a broken heart, however, Jesus did something amazing which seems to be perquisite to having one's own broken heart healed. He asked the Father to forgive those who wronged Him so traumatically.

📖 But Jesus was saying, "*Father, forgive them;* for they do not know what they are doing." Luke 23:34a NASB (Italicized for emphasis).

When people come to the point of faith where they will choose to forgive those who have broken their hearts and leave vengeance in the hand of the Lord, they are able to fully receive the work of Jesus, whose own heart was broken, that their hearts may be made whole.

With the blood and water which flowed from His broken heart, Jesus broke the curse of broken-heartedness to restore joy and wholeness, even to those whose hearts have been broken and fragmented through horrific abuse and trauma.

Jesus not only broke the curse of brokenness and fragmentation, He also won back our wholeness and joy. For years I thought and taught joy was putting Jesus first, others second, and yourself last but Holy Spirit corrected me. He says true joy is Jesus Overflowing You!

Breaking the Curse and Invoking the Blessing:

✝ Jesus, today, by faith, I choose to forgive those who have broken my heart. Vengeance is the Lord's, and I choose to leave judgment in His hands.

✝ In Jesus' Name I apply the blood and water from Jesus' bleeding heart to my own inner brokenness and fragmentation.

✝ I declare I am redeemed from brokenness and fragmentation by the blood of the Lamb out of the hand of the enemy!

✝ I break the curse of broken-heartedness and fragmentation in the Mighty Name of Jesus and through His blood.

✝ I apply the blood and water from Jesus' Bleeding Heart and take back my wholeness!

✝ I break every curse of brokenness and fragmentation and command every demon assigned through that to leave me now in Jesus' Name. (Expel!)

✝ Jesus, I now ask you to bind up the wounds of my broken heart.

✝ Holy Spirit, I invoke Your blessing of the anointing You gave Jesus to heal the broken-hearted.

✝ I invoke Your blessing for my own healing, and so I will be used to release Your healing to others.

✝ Abba Father, in Jesus' Name I invoke the true joy of Jesus Overflowing Me in every aspect of my heart and life.

✝ I invoke Your blessing of wholeness and joy through the blood and water from Jesus' broken heart. Amen.

Endnotes:

[1] Augustus M. Toplady, 1740-1778. Thomas Hasting, 1784-1872; Hymns of Glorious Praise, Gospel Publishing House 1969. Hymn # 336.
[2] Beatles, "All the Lonely People Lyrics on Demand." "http://www.azlyrics.com/lyrics/beatles/eleanorrigby.html
[3] http://www.webmd.com/mental-health/dissociative-identity-disorder-multiple-personality-disorder

MAY HEARTS DARE TO BEAT AGAIN

I wrote a poem in August of 2015 and had it made into bookmarks in December. I share it with a few minor revisions here.

May Hearts Dare to Beat Again

Raped, pillaged, put down, insulted.
Children passed over,
Watching their parent neglect them
While chasing after lovers to
Heal them of their own past neglect.

Somewhere, somehow, the cycle has to stop.
Yet it can never begin to stop,
Until the healing has begun.
To sew up the wounds of the bleeding heart,
And pull together each fragmented part.

Ministers of healing divine yet human,
Must move beneath the surface,
Where the stain of lurking pain,
Makes the heart afraid to beat again.

Oh where can such love be found,
That makes it worth the risk,
To feel the pain and live again?

Could this be the true Gospel Message?
Love so pure, so intimate, and divine.
That one can open the past
And in the future learn
To trust again, love again,
And risk feeling once more?

Yes, this is the hope, the message and ministry,
Of One anointed to heal the broken heart.
The One sent to set the captive free
And set those oppressed at liberty.

Our world, yes probably those reading this,
Is filled with men and women who continue --
Trying to still the pain of abuse
From childhood and beyond.

Sticks and stones may break my bones,
But bones are easily healed.
Curses, neglect, hurtful words
Along with all forms of abuse.
Leave scars that affect all of life,
Until they are gently opened
By the Great Physician's hand.

Only He can heal deep inner wounds,
Hidden from all . . . .
And tucked away deep within.

Only the blood and water
Which flowed from His own broken heart,
Can flow through my broken heart,
To your broken heart,
Until in Him we are whole again.

~Douglas E. Carr 8/17/2015

PRAYING IT ALL THE WAY THROUGH

There are dozens of places to learn more about the seven places Jesus shed His blood to break seven core curses. If you put "Seven places Jesus shed His blood" in an Internet search engine you will find several great articles worth reading.

My Christian life developed with a strong theology of the Word of God. I wanted God to engraft His Word into my heart and save my soul (James 1:21). It took years before I understood theology pertains not only to the Word of God but also to the *God of the Word!*

Over the past few years the God of the Word has quickened His revelation within me concerning how Jesus shed His blood in seven specific places to break seven curses. He has worked in me and through me to invoke God's blessings through Jesus' blood to take back His working to will and to do according to His will. He has shown me how to take back my own health, freedom, prosperity, success, dominion, and wholeness.

This wonderful revelation has become an essential part of nearly every ministry appointment I do. In this chapter I merely want you pray the blood of Jesus over you, and your family, as I have for countless others.

A prayer to apply the wonder of Jesus' blood personally.

Heavenly Father, I am absolutely amazed You love me so much You gave Your Only Begotten Son so I might not perish but have everlasting life.

Jesus, You are the Lamb of God who takes away my sin and gives me power to break curses and invoke blessings through the blood You shed.

I confess I have been selfish, narcissistic, and self-protective. I have built walls around my heart to avoid pain rather than turning to You in my pain.

Jesus, You were tempted in every way I have been, yet were without sin. In the Garden of Gethsemane, You were tempted not to fully surrender to Your Father's will to take our sins upon Yourself on the cross. You asked your best friends to stay awake and pray while you were sorely tempted and traumatized. Every one of them betrayed you.

You prayed, and prayed again "Father, if You are willing, take this cup from Me." You didn't want to be separated from the Father. You didn't want to become sin on our behalf. You were tempted to not be the Lamb of God who takes away the sin of the world.

Thank You for overcoming that temptation and praying "yet not My will but Yours be done." Even with an angel attending You, You began to pray more earnestly, and Your sweat was like drops of blood falling to the ground.

Lord Jesus, I take Your sweat drops of blood and I purposely break the curse of my self-protective, guarded, and self-directed will. I command every spirit of rebellion, every stiff-necked spirit, and every spirit of rejection, fear, and stubbornness to leave me now! (Expel) I use Your blood to break off narcissism from my willing, thinking, and doing.

I invoke Your blessing of God working in me to will and to do of Your good pleasure. Through Your blood I identify with You and say "yet not by will, but Yours be done" in me, by me, and through me.

Jesus, they falsely accused You, tried You unjustly, and tied You to a whipping post. They took a whip embedded with sharp pieces of metal and bone and whipped you, tearing pieces of flesh from Your body.

Isaiah prophesied "by Your stripes I am healed." Peter says we were healed through Your stripes. I confess every place where I and my ancestors have given into sickness. I confess where I have looked to physicians and alternative treatment before looking to You.

Today I take the precious blood from Your stripes and break every curse of sickness, disease, and infirmity. I command every spirit of infirmity and disease to leave me right now in Jesus' Name. (Expel)

In Your Precious Name and through Your Blood, I demolish the stronghold of infirmity and command the root spirit of infirmity to loose me now. (Expel)

I invoke the blessing of health over me and my family line. I pray none of the diseases of Egypt will ever again visit me or my family.

Lord Jesus, Isaiah prophesied You were bruised for my iniquities. You bled underneath the surface of Your skin to break the curse of everything lurking deep within me.

Today, by faith, I apply the blood from Your bruises to break every curse of personal and generational iniquity. I take the blood from Your bruises and break every curse of brokenness, grief, anger, selfishness, sorrow and depression which has held me and my family in bondage. I invoke the blessing of freedom from iniquity, and the blessing of transparency before You and those closest to me.

Jesus, the soldiers added insult to injury when they placed a robe over You, put a staff in Your hands, and crafted a crown of thorns from the symbol of poverty. You became poor for my sake so I might be rich in You. They took the staff from Your hand and beat Your face over and over again. Your blood poured from the wounds on Your head and face.

I confess where I've sought first financial gain rather Your Kingdom. I confess where I have withheld my tithes and offerings and behaved like I alone am responsible for making it financially.

Today, I apply the blood from Your face and head where you wore the crown of thorns, and break every curse of poverty off from me and my family line. I command every spirit of mental poverty to leave me now. (Expel) I invoke Your blessing of prosperity over my life. I ask You to bless me financially and use me to bless Your work and Your people financially. I invoke Your blessing so I may prosper in all things even as my soul prospers.

Jesus, they led you to the cross. They nailed Your hands to the tree. They took Your hands that healed the sick, multiplied the loaves and fishes, comforted the hurting, and did the creative work of God. Soldiers nailed Your precious hands to the cross. You could barely pull Yourself up to take a breath when you were suffocating there. Thank You, Jesus!

Today, by faith, I apply the blood from Your hands and break every curse against my success and the work of my hands. I command every spirit of sabotage and unrelenting destruction to leave me now. (Expel) By Your blood, I break every curse of illegitimacy and command spirits working illegitimacy to leave me now. (Expel)

Father, through the blood from Jesus' hands I invoke Your blessing over my hands and my work. I pray You will bless me and help me to work at whatever I do with all my heart as working for the Lord, and not just men. I ask you to release Your authority for healing, deliverance, and anointing through my hands.

Jesus, Your feet carried You everywhere Your Father sent You. You did not worry about provision for Your journey. You just went to the places Father would show You. You walked on the water. You took dominion over demons, disease, injustice, and poverty.

You tread upon the lion and the serpent. You trampled the great lion and the dragon, but they nailed Your feet to the cross.

I can picture You hanging there; the heaviness of our sin and weight of Your own body suffocating You as You hung there. When You tried pushing up by Your feet to catch a breath, the pain was unbearable. Blood poured from the nail wounds. I now apply that blood and cast off every spirit working against my dominion and authority. (Expel)

Jesus, You did this for me! How wonderful, how marvelous is Your love for me. Today, by faith, I apply the blood from Your feet, and break every curse against my dominion, power, and authority.

Through Your blood I invoke Father's blessing of dominion, power, and authority over sin, first in my own life and then in the world around me. With Jesus' authority I will be sent as Father sent Jesus. Lord Jesus, I receive Your commission by faith and I will forcibly advance your Kingdom on earth as it is in heaven.

Jesus, most precious to me is the blood and water flowing from Your own broken heart. I confess my own brokenness and lay my heart condition open before you. By faith I apply the water and blood from Your broken heart and break every curse of brokenness and fragmentation off me and my descendants.

I speak to every demon causing fragmentation and resist you in Jesus' Name and through His blood. Loose me now! (Expel)

Father, through the blood and water from Jesus' broken heart, I invoke Your blessing of wholeness and joy over my life. May Jesus overflow through me in everything I think, say, and do.

I now declare I am crucified with Christ and I no longer live, but Christ lives through me. The life I live in the body, I live by faith in the Son of God, who loved me and gave Himself for me.

THE DEVIL'S ATTEMPT
TO OBSCURE THE POWER OF THE BLOOD

For centuries the devil has tried to steal, kill, and destroy the Church by moving it away from the blood of the Passover Lamb. Many can remember how central the blood of Jesus used to be in worship. I became a Christian in 1972 and memorized songs we often sang in the church I attended as well as in the five churches I've pastored. Consider the lyrics of some of the songs which used to be common across denominational lines. The first one begins with the question only the blood of Jesus can answer.

Nothing but the Blood

What can wash away my sin?
Nothing but the *blood of Jesus*;
What can make me whole again?
Nothing but the *blood of Jesus*. (Chorus)

Chorus:
Oh! precious is the flow
That makes me white as snow;
No other fount I know,
Nothing but the *blood of Jesus*.

For my pardon, this I see,
Nothing but the *blood of Jesus*;
For my cleansing this my plea,
Nothing but the *blood of Jesus*. (Repeat Chorus)

Nothing can for sin atone,
Nothing but the *blood of Jesus*;
Naught of good that I have done,

Nothing but the *blood of Jesus*. (Repeat Chorus)
This is all my hope and peace,
Nothing but the *blood of Jesus*;
This is all my righteousness,
Nothing but the *blood of Jesus*. (Repeat Chorus)

Now by this I'll overcome—
Nothing but the *blood of Jesus*,
Now by this I'll reach my home—
Nothing but the *blood of Jesus*. (Repeat Chorus)

Glory! Glory! This I sing—
Nothing but the *blood of Jesus*,
All my praise for this I bring—
Nothing but the *blood of Jesus*. (Repeat Chorus)[1]
(Italicized for emphasis)

The second is a Gospel song that has always been close to my heart.

Victory in Jesus

Verse one:
I heard an old, old story,
How a Savior came from glory,
How He gave His life on Calvary
To save a wretch like me;
I heard about His groaning,
Of his precious blood atoning,
Then I repented of my sins;
And won the victory.

Chorus:
O victory in Jesus,
My Savior, forever.
He sought me and bought me
With His redeeming blood;
He loved me ere I knew Him,
And all my love is due Him,
He plunged me to victory,
Beneath the cleansing flood[2] (Italicized for emphasis)

The third song underscores how the blood of Jesus used to be a major focus within worship.

There's Power in the Blood

Would you be free from your burden of sin?
There's power in the blood, power in the blood
Would you o'er evil the victory win?
There's wonderful power in the blood

Chorus:
There is power, power, wonder-working power
In the blood of the Lamb
There is power, power, wonder-working power
In the precious blood of the Lamb

Would you be free from your passion and Pride?
There's power in the *blood*, power in the *blood*.
Come for a cleansing to Calvary's tide;
There's wonderful power in the *blood*. (Repeat Chorus)

Would you be whiter, much whiter than snow?
There's power in the blood, power in the blood
Sin stains are lost in its life-giving flow
There's wonderful power in the blood. (Repeat Chorus)

Would you do service for Jesus, your King?
There's power in the blood, power in the blood
Would you live daily His praises to sing?
There's wonderful power in the blood. (Repeat Chorus)[3]
(Italicized for emphasis)

The devil's attempt to divert attention away from the blood certainly did not begin with seeker sensitive worship. He did his best to see Jesus killed before He was nailed to the cross. Many Jews believed the Messiah would appear at the pinnacle of the Temple, but Satan tempted Jesus to throw himself off that pinnacle which could have resulted in death apart from the cross (Matthew 4:5-7).

Later, the devil stirred the people in the synagogue with such fury over Jesus's works they tried to take Him to the brow of the hill in order to throw him down the cliff, but He escaped the devil's attempt to kill Him apart from the cross (Luke 4:28-30).

You may wonder why the devil was so bent on Jesus dying before He made it to the cross on Passover. It is because Satan hates the blood of Jesus which was shed on Calvary's Cross. He hates that it can save you. He hates that it can heal you, deliver you, and break every curse if only you apply it. He doesn't want you or me to realize how much power is in the blood of Jesus.

Jesus had to die on Passover and His death should be observed on Passover. Jesus had to die on a cross in order to offer us remission from curses for "cursed is everyone who hands on a tree." Paul explains this by quoting from Deuteronomy. Take a look.

📖 "If a man has committed a sin deserving of death, and he is put to death, and you hang him on a tree, his body shall not remain overnight on the tree, but you shall surely bury him that day, so that you do not defile the land which the Lord your God is giving you as an inheritance; *for he who is hanged is accursed of God.* Deuteronomy 21:22-23 (Italicized for emphasis).

📖 *Christ has redeemed us from the curse of the law, having become a curse for us* (for it is written, "Cursed is everyone who hangs on a tree"), that the blessing of Abraham might come upon the Gentiles in Christ Jesus, that we might receive the promise of the Spirit through faith. Galatians 3:13-14 (Italicized for emphasis).

If the devil can't divert our attention from the cross, he will try to limit the focus of Jesus' blood to salvation alone. I have memorized dozens of Scriptures over the years, including a few entire chapters. There is one verse, however, that I memorized so incorrectly that I had to check it out in every translation I have.

I asked our people in our church and at a jail service to finish this statement, and nearly everyone "quoted it" incorrectly. Let's see how you do. Finish this verse from Hebrews 9:22 "Without the shedding of blood there is no what?" The way I memorized it was "Without the shedding of blood there is no remission *of sin.*" That is incorrect! It limits Jesus' blood to salvation, when it was also shed to break every curse and bring healing.

Some Bibles say "Without the shedding of blood there is no forgiveness of sins," but five out of six of my favorite translations correctly read "Without the shedding of blood there is no remission." I am convinced that is the best translation. Without the shedding of blood there is no remission PERIOD!

In the scope of *From Woe is Me to Wow is He,* the shedding of Jesus' blood includes remission from the curses of: a selfish, narcissistic, or self-protective will; sickness and disease; personal and generational iniquitous patterns; poverty; and the curses against: productivity and creativity; dominion and authority. Thankfully it also includes remission from the curse of fragmentation, dissociation, and brokenness. There is remission of these curses by the blood of Jesus IF and when it is applied. It is no wonder the devil doesn't want us to know the power of the blood of Jesus.

The first and last books of the Bible share how integral the shedding of blood is to Christian life and victory. Revelation 13:8 speaks of Jesus as the Lamb who was slain from the foundation of the world. Jesus dying on the cross at Passover was always God's plan. He knew what Adam and Eve would do. He knew our need long before we had it! He loves people so much He had a plan of remission for people of the Old Testament, New Testament, and now! Even before Jesus went to the cross Father Abraham believed and it was counted to him as righteousness!

God's first use of innocent blood was demonstrated after Adam sinned. I actually think we will see Adam and Eve in heaven – not because of what they did, but because of what God did when he made garments of skin to cover their shame and nakedness.

Adam and Eve tried to cover themselves with fig leaves. They are less than 4 x 7 inches and irregular like a maple leaf. They're even smaller than grape leaves! Can you picture them trying to cover their nakedness by sowing fig leaves together? I wonder if that is why Jesus cursed the fig tree even though it wasn't the season for ripe figs (See Mark 11:12-14). Could He have been thinking back to when Adam and Eve tried to cover their sin and shame apart from faith in remission through the shedding of blood?

When Adam sinned, God killed an innocent animal. Blood was shed for remission of guilt and for redemption. God saved Adam and Eve on the credit plan – the down payment was the blood of an animal – the payment in full is Jesus blood!

There is nothing else in all creation that can bring remission. There is nothing people can do to earn remission. Without the shedding of blood there is no remission. In the Garden of Eden God sacrificed an innocent animal to make clothes of skin for Adam and Eve. This pointed to the sacrifice of Jesus, the Lamb of God who takes away the sin of the world.

The Passover is a better picture of how the blood of Jesus works. The book of Exodus begins with the Hebrew people in bondage to Egypt. The Egyptians worshipped all the wrong gods, and the plagues were judgment against demon gods and those who worshipped them. (You can study this in Exodus chapters 7-12.)

The ten plagues were God's judgments against idolatrous worship. The first three plagues affected everyone in the land. The land of Goshen, where the Hebrews lived, was spared from the next six plagues. The final plague was the death of the first born of every family and flock – unless God's instruction about Passover blood was believed enough to be followed by faith.

The Passover was instituted to protect people of faith from the plague of the firstborn. Even though the head of the Jewish Year occurs in late autumn, God told Moses that the month of Nissan (March and April in the Julian calendar) would be the first month of the year. Some believe this parallels the time a baby spends in its mother's womb before being born. I wonder if it shows how life really begins once you experience the power of Passover. The blood of the Passover Lamb saves us from the evil one who wills to kill, steal, and destroy. It brings us into abundant life!

At Passover the people were told to take a one-year-old male lamb without defect and slaughter it at twilight. They were to pour some of the blood of the lamb and put it on the sides and tops of the doorframes of the houses where the lambs were to be eaten. The motion of touching the sides and tops of the doorframes symbolize the cross.

God commanded His people to commemorate this Passover annually for the generations to come. God never wants His people to forget about the power of the blood, but Satan hates the blood.

The early Church focused on the blood of Jesus. On the day of Pentecost, the Holy Spirit fell on 120 people, by the end of the day God added more than 3,000 people to the Church! Within one year it tripled in size. The Church quickly spread from city to city and region to region as Believers preached the death, burial, and resurrection of Jesus Christ.

Think of the power of the early church to heal the sick, cast out demons, win the lost, equip the saved, and bring transformation to wealthy but pagan cities like Antioch and Ephesus. The church was able to change the moral climate of places like Ephesus and Corinth through preaching, teaching, and signs and wonders. Thousands were added daily to the Church because its members understood there's power, power, wonder working power in the blood of the Lamb.

Satan went to war against the blood! The Council of Nicea I was convened in 325 (AD) by Constantine, Emperor of the Roman Empire. Constantine, a worshipper of the sun-god, claimed he 'converted' to Christianity. What he really did was "married" the church to pagan worship of the sun, even changing the date of Easter to coincide with celebration of the Teutonic goddess of Spring, Eastre.

Constantine's reign marked the alliance of state and church. Christians were no longer persecuted by the pagans. Instead, Christians persecuted others (including other Christians) with a zeal and a vengeance that would shock the pagans. More Christians were killed by other Christians in the first century after the Council of Nicea than had been killed by pagans in the century before Nicea.

Just one year after convening the Council of Nicea, Constantine had his own son Crispus put to death. Later he suffocated his wife Fausta in an overheated bath. Then he had his sister's son flogged to death and her husband strangled. It was also during the reign of Constantine that the cross became a sacred symbol in Christianity, just as it had been in pagan religions. (You can study how the cross was used in pagan worship on your own.)

Constantine was used to separate the Passover message from the resurrection of Jesus. In 2016 most Churches celebrated Easter on March 27. Jesus was crucified on Passover which was April 22 in 2016. How can it be that Jesus' death and burial was being celebrated 4 weeks after His resurrection? It is because Constantine aligned celebration of the resurrection of Christ with the celebration of the son god and named it Eastre after the sun god.

What happened to Passover?

The Council of Antioch CE 345 said anyone celebrating the blood on Passover would be removed from the church and considered cursed.

The Council of Laodicea CE 365 decreed anyone taking part in Jewish festivals would be cursed, as would anyone who observed the Sabbath.

The Council of AGDE, France CE 506 said ministers could not take part in Jewish festivals.

The Council of Toledo X seventh century said Easter must be celebrated uniformly at the time set by the Nicea decree rather than at the time of the Passover.

The Council of Nicea II forbid anyone who secretly or openly observed the Sabbath to be part of the Church.

The devil has done everything he can do to make Christians anemic apart from the power of the blood of the Passover Lamb.

I have taught on the power of the blood of Jesus to break curses brought upon us by the first Adam and invoke blessings redeemed for us by the 2nd Adam. We need to get this message! We need to bring our wills, health, character, finances, work of our hands, dominion, and wholeness into full alignment with what Jesus wills for us – and it will take application of the power of the blood to do it.

Do not consider this done if you are not willing and doing fully according to God's will. Do not consider this done if sickness is reigning in your home. Do not consider this done if you are struggling with the same bad attitudes or stinking thinking as your ancestors. Do not consider this done if you are still struggling financially. Do not consider this done if the work of your hands isn't blessed beyond your imagination. Do not consider this done if you do not have dominion and authority over sin, the devil, and circumstances. Do not consider this done if you are still walking in brokenness.

The blood of Jesus must be applied in order to find remission of sin and to break the power of curses. Think back to the original Passover. Notice how some verses from Exodus 12 point to the Lamb of God who went to the cross.

📖 Now the Lord spoke to Moses and Aaron in the land of Egypt, saying, 2 "This month shall be your beginning of months; it shall be the first month of the year to you. *(Your whole life starts over when you learn to apply the blood!)* 3 Speak to all the congregation of Israel, saying: 'On the tenth of this month every man shall take for himself a lamb, according to the house of his father, a lamb for a household. Exodus 12:1-3 NKJV. *(Parenthesis and italics mine throughout this section)*

📖 5 Your lamb shall be without blemish, a male of the first year. You may take it from the sheep or from the goats. 6 Now you shall keep it until the fourteenth day of the same month. Then the whole assembly of the congregation of Israel shall kill it at twilight. Exodus 12:5-6 NKJV. *(Jesus, the perfect Lamb of God was crucified on Passover!)*

📖 7 And they shall take some of the blood and put it on the two doorposts and on the lintel of the houses where they eat it. Exodus 12:7 NKJV. *(Blood applied in the sign of a cross!)*

📖 For I will pass through the land of Egypt on that night, and will strike all the firstborn in the land of Egypt, both man and beast; and against all the gods of Egypt I will execute judgment: I am the Lord. Exodus 12:12 NKJV. *(People who do not apply the blood of Jesus come under judgment and curse)*

📖 13 Now the blood shall be a sign for you on the houses where you are. And when I see the blood, I will pass over you; and the plague shall not be on you to destroy you when I strike the land of Egypt. Exodus 12:13 NKJV.

God wants to "Pass over" the judgment you and I deserve. He wants us to be free from the power of death and the curse. He wants us to enjoy abundant life. But if those Fathers in Exodus would not have applied the blood by faith, every first born in their home and in their herds and flocks would have died! God doesn't want you or your children to come under judgment and die. Apply the blood! Put your faith in Jesus and His blood. There's power, power, wonder working power in the precious blood of the Lamb.

Prayer:

† Father, through faith in the precious Name of Jesus Christ, I apply the blood of Jesus Christ to my life, my home, my family and my all.
† I apply His blood to my mind, will, emotions and memories.
† I apply His blood to who I am and who I want to be for you.
† I apply the blood of Jesus to my health, finances, ministry, work, thought life and living this day by faith.
† I thank you for the blood.
† I am redeemed by the blood of the Lamb from the hand of the enemy. Amen.

Endnotes:

[1]*Nothing but the Blood.* Words & Music: Robert Lowry, Public Domain.
[2]*Victory in Jesus,* Eugene M. Barlett, 1885-1941. Public Domain.
[3]*There is Power in the Blood*, Lewis E. Jones, 1865-1936. Public Domain.

ADDENDUM:
TREE OF LIFE VERSUS TREE OF KNOWLEDGE

The Lord has chosen to set up His habitation in you and me through His Holy Spirit. He wants Kingdom people to advance His Kingdom through the power of the blood! We are to feed on the Tree of Life rather than the tree of the knowledge of good and evil.

God does move into dark places to shine His light. In the first book of the Bible we see Him entering chaos to bring Divine Order. God still resides in and through people who flow from the Tree of Life, rather than from the tree of the knowledge of good and evil.

Jesus is the way, the truth and life. His Spirit is the stream of living water flowing from the Tree of Life. If we want Him to dwell among us, we must open our secret closets and come out of hiding and pretension and learn to worship God in Spirit and reality.

Let's begin with the Bible's first and final mention of the Tree of Life.

📖 And out of the ground the Lord God made every tree grow that is pleasant to the sight and good for food. The *tree of life* was also in the midst of the garden, and the tree of the knowledge of good and evil. Genesis 2:9 (Italicized for emphasis).

📖 In the middle of its street, and on either side of the river, was the *tree of life*, which bore twelve fruits, each tree yielding its fruit every month. The leaves of the tree were for the healing of the nations. Revelation 22:2 (Italicized for emphasis).

God instructed Adam and Eve to enjoy the Tree of Life and avoid the tree of knowledge. As you know, they failed and gave into the devil's temptation. They ate fruit from the tree of the knowledge of good and evil. So have I, how about you? Knowledge in itself is good, but when knowledge come through soulish and self-centered thinking, it becomes evil because it leaves God out of the equation.

I lived the first 20 years of my Christian life wallowing in the tree of the knowledge of good and evil. One sad part of being in the tree of knowledge is you doesn't realize when you are feeding from it.

God gave me a dream while I was working on this to remind me of what life was like when I lived and ministered from the tree of knowledge. I dreamt of when my children were ten and under, and I was their father, their pastor, and the founding principal of their Christian school. The school started small and my children made up 25% of the school body.

My dream was a play back of when one student left his wallet in a bathroom and someone helped themselves to a couple of dollars that was in it. I called the school together and tried to scare the culprit into a confession. No one confessed, however, so I went to Hebrews 12 and warned how God disciplines His children as severely as He needs to so they will repent. I then led them in prayer, asking God to take out His whip and punish the guilty one until they repented.

One teacher's aide took me aside and gently rebuked me for using God to scare the children. I justified myself stating the fear of the Lord is the beginning of wisdom.

Imagine my woe and shame when the guilty party finally came forward. It was one of my own children! I promptly dealt with the issue, and confession and restitution were made, but I began judging myself as harshly as I did the one who took the money. I figured God wanted to "catch me" and punish me like I wanted to catch the "thief" and punish him.

I actually called the chairman of the church board and told him I needed to step down as pastor. It was obvious to me I didn't rule my own household well. I didn't want to bring reproach upon the church because of my failure to raise godly children. Thankfully the chairman helped me realize I had not totally failed as a parent and God wasn't through with me or my children. Since I lived in the tree of knowledge, I couldn't comprehend God's grace flowing from the Tree of Life.

I began to understand the Tree of Life when I took a class from Ted Haggard on *Leading Life Giving Churches* and much of what he taught has shaped my life and is probably evident in the message I try to live and share. I realize Ted fell, I actually wept when he did as I prayed for him, his family, and church. I am grateful God answered my prayers and has restored him and is using him.

Since being introduced to the Tree of Life, I want to live there. I seem to have a "monkey anointing," however, jumping from the tree of life to the tree of knowledge of good and evil, even though the fruit of the Tree of Life is far more satisfying.

We need to realize both God and Satan are at the door. God wills to bring us fully into the Tree of Life. Satan is still tempting people to live and bear fruit from the tree of knowledge of good and evil.

Let's compare the fruit of the Tree of Life and the tree of the knowledge of good and evil. I have preached on this subject several times and actually cannot remember how much of it I gleaned from "*Leading Life Giving Churches*" and how much I've learned by living in the tree of life since. For sake of brevity I will abbreviate tree of life as "TOL," and the tree of the knowledge of good and evil as "TOK."

Note, knowledge in itself is good, but when knowledge flows through a soulish nature its fruit is not good.

Living in the TOL is all about remaining in Jesus and abiding in Him. It focuses on relationship and communion with the Lord. Life in the TOK centers around religion and rules and focuses more on outward appearance than on issues of the heart.

People living in the TOL desire to draw nearer to God and His manifest presence. As they draw nearer to God together, they know they will be closer to Him and one another. People in the TOK jockey for position. Like the early disciples, they are concerned about who will be given the highest honor and position.

People in the TOL pursue love, which comes from a pure heart, a good conscience, and a sincere faith. People in the TOK are concerned about titles, recognition, and being honored and respected.

People in the TOL humble themselves and look for ways to serve. People in the TOK exalt themselves and want to be served and honored as leaders, pastors, apostles, prophets, or whatever.

People in the TOL bear the fruit of childlike innocence and are fun and unpretentious. Fruit from the TOK looks good, acts good, but leaves a nasty taste in your mouth.

The TOL produces vulnerability and people feel safe and willing to confess their sins to one another and pray for each other. People swinging from the TOK build walls of protection and secrecy around their hearts. They are guarded and tend to hold others at arm's distance.

People living in the TOL feel valued and value one another apart from performance. People in the TOK attempt to earn love and perform in order to win approval, and expect others to do the same.

Speaking of value, consider how purchase price sets value. If you try to buy or sell a house, there is the asking price, what the seller is willing to sell it for, and what a buyer is willing to pay for it. In the end, the buyer and seller set the value of a house by what the buyer is willing to pay for it, and the seller is willing to sell it for. In light of setting value, consider what God was willing to pay for our redemption!

God the Father and God the Son set our value by what They were willing to pay to redeem us. Our heavenly father so loved us, He sacrificed his only begotten Son on our behalf. Jesus so loved us, He gave His all and carried the cross we deserved. People in the TOL recognize how much God values every person.

In the TOL grace stands for favor. Grace demonstrates how God willingly paid the price because we are worth it to Him. In the TOK grace means unmerited favor, treating people as worthless and thinking God rescued us out of pity rather than love. When people truly respond to the grace and favor of the Lord, He gives them the desire and the power to do His will.

The TOL leads to life and fruitfulness. Fruit comes from abiding in Jesus, and even more so, from His abiding in us. The TOK leads to legalism and trying to earn our way into God's favor.

The TOL leads to increased anointing. Preaching is much easier for me since I've been in the TOL, because it flows not only from what God said, but also from what He is saying. The TOK leads to self-effort. I remember reading eight, ten, or even more commentaries for every sermon, trying to find something that sounded good. I was able to preach the best of man's wisdom, but usually spent 12-20 hours preparing every sermon. In the TOL I'm learning to let God speak through me and sermons come in less than half the time with far greater impact.

The TOL leads to flow. When you walk in the TOL, Holy Spirit's anointing flows through you to meet the needs of people. You may feel power go out, and may even need to rest, but there is great satisfaction ministering in the flow. The TOK leads to frustration, which may explain why so many preachers leave the ministry.

The TOL brings a sense of worth and value. People in the TOL value themselves and others because they realize God does. The TOK brings a sense of worthlessness concerning self and others.

The TOL increases one's sense of worth. People value themselves and others when they observe from life, rather than judgment. The TOK leads to self-rejection and rejecting others.

The TOL proclaims the year of God's favor because the Spirit of the Living God flows from the TOL. The TOK proclaims God's judgment. People living from the TOL can win the drunkard, the tax collector, and the woman caught in adultery because they value people. People in the TOK simply preach judgment, hoping people may see how worthless they are so they might turn to Jesus.

The TOL believes God wants happy children so badly He sent Jesus to give them abundant life. How can we ever imagine the abundant life includes being miserable? The TOK makes people miserable as it preaches judgment and how God turns from sinful people.

The TOL knows God is out to bless me and others. The TOK believes God is out to get me. The TOK views God as a great policeman in the sky trying to catch people doing something wrong so He can punish them.

My entire perspective of the Lord and myself was transformed when I understood God calling out to Adam and Eve from a TOL perspective. I always thought God called out "Where are you?" so He could find Adam and punish him. I'm sure my upbringing had something to do with this.

When I was a boy I was forbidden to walk down the railroad tracks from our home to the river. Once, however, my alcoholic grandfather took me by the wrist and forced me to go to the river with him, even though I resisted and cried out I wasn't supposed to go there. My Dad soon discovered I was missing and headed straight to the river. When he found me, he grabbed me by the wrist and dragged me home, swatting me on the behind with his belt nearly every step of the way.

I didn't know my Dad had dreamed of finding one of us kids lying face down in the river. I assumed he came after me and punished me because he didn't love me and wanted to hurt me. I wrongly viewed God the same way as I did my father when I lived in the TOK.

God already knew where and why Adam and Eve were hiding! He didn't call out to them so He could find them and spank them. He called out to them so they might confess where they were and own up to what they had done, so He could forgive them and cleanse them of all unrighteousness. He actually clothed them with cloaks of skin, meaning the blood of innocent animals was shed on their behalf.

People in the Tree of Life focus on correction, rather than punishment, because they understand God's heart. God wants to correct His children because they are worth it to Him. The TOK views people as worthless and only deserving punishment.

I've preached at the Branch County Jail once a month since 1988. I began under the late Chaplain Jerry Vercrysse who truly lived from the Tree of Life. He often asked how certain people were doing. When I had to give a poor report he always said "Don't give up on them, aren't you glad Jesus never gave up on you?" That is how people are viewed from the TOL. They share the heart of the Good Shepherd and the prodigal son's father.

The TOL is life-giving while the TOK is more concerned about right and wrong. Sadly, I confess I reared my children from the Tree of Knowledge rather than the Tree of Life. I worked primarily from the TOK as a pastor as well as the principal of a Christian school. All those precious children, now adults, would have been much better served had I flowed from the TOL.

The Tree of Life develops a culture of innocence in which people can be transparent and unashamed, fully assured of God's love, acceptance, and forgiveness. The Tree of Knowledge develops a culture of shame which tries to earn approval and favor from God and man.

As demonstrated by the Pharisees, the TOK carries the attitude "get away from me you dirty sinner." Jesus, on the other hand, demonstrated the attitude "come unto me all you who are weary, and I will give you rest." He came to seek the lost and to offer Himself as physician for those in need rather than for those who thought they were well. Mark illustrates this comparison between the Pharisees and Jesus.

📖 Now it happened, as He was dining in Levi's house, that many tax collectors and sinners also sat together with Jesus and His disciples; for there were many, and they followed Him. And when the scribes and Pharisees saw Him eating with the tax collectors and sinners, they said to His disciples, "How is it that He eats and drinks with tax collectors and sinners?" When Jesus heard it, He said to them, "Those who are well have no need of a physician, but those who are sick. *I did not come to call the righteous, but sinners, to repentance.*" Mark 2:15-17 (Italicized for emphasis).

A very practical example of this comes from how we treat people caught in questionable behaviors like smoking, for example. People living in the tree of life smile and greet a smoker, while people living in the TOK scowl at a smoker. I remember a dear man, an Elder in one church, who had a lot of great qualities, but living from the Tree of Life was not one of them. We were sharing lunch in a nice restaurant when a person sitting a couple of tables away lit a cigarette. The Elder began coughing in an exaggerated manner while trying to wave the smoke away. He valued his right to eat in a smoke free environment more than he did the person. His contempt for the person spoke louder than the thunderous prayer he offered before lunch.

People in the TOL move through the Holy Spirit who always manifests love, joy, peace, patience, and the like. People in the TOK move through the flesh. They are quick to condemn, unlike Jesus is quick to say "Neither do I condemn you, go and sin no more."

The tree of life pardons, but the tree of knowledge condemns. The TOL produces genuine guilt which leads to confession and right relationship, while the TOK releases shame that leads to hiding sin and failure.

I personally lived with a stronghold of shame for over twenty years. I judged myself from the tree of the knowledge of good and evil because of things I did years ago when I lived in the tree of knowledge. There were others, including those I sacrificed so much for, who judged me from the TOK and reinforced the impression I was beyond redemption and not worth saving.

I was released from the stronghold of shame after learning true guilt leads to confession, repentance and life. Guilt says "I *did* something bad" and makes confession leading to God's forgiveness and cleansing. Shame, on the other hand, believes "I *am* bad and worthless," and makes one feel too dirty to approach God.

The TOL brings conviction leading to confession and repentance. The TOK brings condemnation which loses all hope of ever being able to change. The TOL points to a loving God while the TOK points to an angry God.

In the Tree of Life people can receive love, acceptance and forgiveness because they are drawn to the love of God and the love of His people. Tree of Knowledge people try to look good in hopes of earning love, acceptance, and forgiveness.

In the Tree of Life people can run into God's arms, but in the Tree of Knowledge they are victims, too full of shame to even approach God. Such is often true of people who were molested or abused as children. They often view themselves as so dirty and shameful they don't think God even wants to be near them. Part of deep healing ministry helps them transition to the Tree of Life. Once there, they finally realize Jesus was and is right there with them, with His arms stretched out to welcome and comfort them. The TOL believes "Just as I am without one plea, but that thy blood was shed for me." The TOK offers "Take my works and leave me be."

The Tree of Life presents the Bible as the Word of Life. The TOK uses it as a two edged sword to cut people down. The TOL helps people come clean with no more secrets. The TOK seems to believe everything is fine and dandy as long as no one discovers your secrets.

In the Tree of Life, you *believe* and become increasingly like Jesus. In the TOK you *do* and try to become like Jesus but end up more like the Pharisees of old. The TOL appeals to those craving true relationship while the TOK appeals to those seeking the "stability" and familiarity of religion.

The Tree of Life oozes life while the TOK oozes death. The TOL pulls others near while the TOK pushes people away. Knowledge in the TOL opens hearts to receive spiritual revelation. Knowledge from the TOK puffs up and cannot receive revelation from Holy Spirit through blinded spiritual eyes. The TOL produces repentance and hope, but the TOK brings hopelessness and despair.

Let's take a closer look at how Adam and Eve fell short of the Tree of Life and ended up in the tree of the knowledge of good and evil.

It was Adam's refusal to own up to what he did and who he became (a sinner) that turned away God's correction and blessing, and brought God's curse and punishment. Of course, sin does need to be dealt with, and there are consequences to our actions, but *after* Adam and Eve sinned, God took an innocent life and blood was shed in order to present Adam and Eve with a covering of sacrifice to replace the ineffective leaves they used to cover their sin, shame and nakedness. The very first sin engaged God's love to make the very first sacrifice of innocent blood to present a pardon for sin.

Disobedience, then and now, brings a curse and separates people from the Tree of Life. We have already considered the first curse people inherited from Adam and Eve when they disobeyed God and ate from the wrong tree. Eating from the knowledge of good and evil drives us away from God even as it did Adam and Eve.

📖 Then to Adam He said, "Because you have heeded the voice of your wife, and have eaten from the tree of which I commanded you,

📖 saying, 'You shall not eat of it': "Cursed is the ground for your sake; In toil you shall eat of it All the days of your life. Genesis 3:17.

Adam was driven from the garden not only because he sinned, but also because he hid, blamed, and denied rather than confessing sin.

📖 So he drove out the man; and he placed at the east of the garden of Eden Cherubims, and a flaming sword which turned every way, to keep the way of the tree of life. Genesis 3:24.

Our sin pushes God away but His love draws us near. His only requirement is that we own up and confess sin so we can repent and turn from it. Consider some verses which speak of confession and its link to wholeness.

📖 Whoever conceals their sins does not prosper, but the one who confesses and renounces them finds mercy. Proverbs 28:13 NIV.

I lived in the tree of knowledge for years. I did my very best to present a good front so no one would suspect the sin, pain, and self-rejection lurking in my heart. I wanted to look good so God and others might love and accept me. The Bible way, however, is confessing and renouncing sin.

King David was miserable until his friend Nathan loved him enough to confront him concerning his sin (see Psalm 51). I believe it was through confrontation and earnest confession and repentance David was able to testify of the Lord's goodness in Psalm 32.

📖 I acknowledged my sin to You, and my iniquity I have not hidden. I said, "I will confess my transgressions to the Lord," and You forgave the iniquity of my sin. Selah. Psalm 32:5.

Thank God for true friends who love enough to confront sin!

In Acts 19 the sons of Sceva tried to minister deliverance from the tree of knowledge rather than the tree of life and an evil spirit jumped on them, overpowered them and gave them such a beating that they ran out of the house naked and believing. The people who witnessed their failure finally realized how some minister out of the anointing and others from the flesh.

As individuals and churches we need to purposely reject the tree of the knowledge of good and evil and return to the Tree of Life. Let me outline a few steps to move from the TOK to the TOL.

The first step is stretching your hand forth and grasping the Tree of life. Adam and Eve were barred from the tree of life and its life-giving fruit. I truly wonder if things would have been different had they confessed "Lord, we are hiding because we sinned." I realize innocent blood was shed to make Adam and Eve coats of skin, but perhaps they didn't invoke the blessing of sacrifice, even though the Lord offered it. God made them garments of skin, but they did not wear them by faith. They looked better on the outside but weren't clean on the inside.

Jesus is the Tree of Life. It's not enough to just touch him, we need to take hold of him, and remain in him. Adam and Eve failed to do so and lost their ability to live forever in the flesh.

📖 Then the Lord God said, "Behold, the man has become like one of Us, to know good and evil. And now, lest he put out his hand and take also of the tree of life, and eat, and live forever"— therefore the Lord God *sent him out* of the garden of *Eden to till the ground from which he was taken.* So He drove out the man; and He placed cherubim at the east of the garden of Eden, and a flaming sword which turned every way, to guard the way to the tree of life. Genesis 3:22-24 (Italicized for emphasis).

It is interesting Adam was driven out of the garden back to *the place from which he was taken.* This makes me think of people who fall away from God's gracious gifts and go back to their old lifestyles apart from Christ.

Paul calls the Galatians foolish for doing this in Galatians 3:1-4. Hebrews 5:5:11-14 warns against people falling away.

I believe such passages describe people who begin their salvation in the tree of life but slip back into tree of knowledge with human knowledge, efforts, and good works.

Since Jesus is the Tree of Life, in Him we take back the ability to live forever. Eternal life is eternal! Jesus died on the cross so we might not perish but have eternal life. But we need to stay connected to the Vine. Consider Jesus' words.

📖 Abide in Me, and I in you. As the branch cannot bear fruit of itself, unless it abides in the vine, neither can you, unless you abide in Me. "I am the vine, you are the branches. *He who abides in Me, and I in him, bears much fruit*; for without Me you can do nothing. John 15:4-5 (Italicized for emphasis).

Abiding in Jesus means remaining in the Tree of Life. When we remain in the tree of life we will bear much fruit. Apart from vital connection with Jesus we can do nothing of eternal value.

The second step is seeking heavenly wisdom. James mentions there are two kinds of wisdom, heavenly which flows from heaven: and unspiritual earthly which is from the devil. Heavenly wisdom is tree of life wisdom. It brings the ability to see things from God's point of view. Proverbs equates such wisdom as a tree of life for those who take hold of it.

📖 Happy is the man who finds wisdom, and the man who gains understanding; For her proceeds are better than the profits of silver, and her gain than fine gold. She is more precious than rubies, and all the things you may desire cannot compare with her. Length of days is in her right hand, in her left hand riches and honor. Her ways are ways of pleasantness, and all her paths are peace. *She is a tree of life to those who take hold of her*, and happy are all who retain her. Proverbs 3:13-18 (Italicized for emphasis).

Wisdom chooses to live by faith from the Tree of Life, rather than by flesh from the Tree of Knowledge. Wisdom makes open confession by faith, rather than hiding and covering the stinky flesh. Wisdom surrenders and submits by faith, rather than hanging on to personal rights, pride, and living according to the sinful nature. Wisdom crucifies personal rights and actively seeks to follow and obey Jesus and that, in turn, breaks the power of the curse and opens the door to blessing.

Step three is seeking first the Kingdom of God and His righteousness.

Jesus tells us if we truly surrender to the rule and reign of the Kingdom (King's domain), we can enjoy abundant life like Adam and Eve did before they fell by eating from the tree of the knowledge of good and evil. The fruit of seeking first the Kingdom and His righteousness comes from the tree of life (see Matthew 6:33). Look at the following wisdom from Proverbs.

📖 The fruit of the righteous is a tree of life . . . Proverbs 11:30a.

Righteousness means being in right standing with God through confession, repentance and being justified through the blood of Jesus. It also includes being at the right place, at the right time, with the right people, doing the right things under the direction of God.

God makes us righteous when we trust Him enough to make honest confession, move on in true repentance, and continue in true obedience through abiding in Jesus.

Step four is to cut off perverse speech and invite wholesome people to speak into and over you.

Jesus said we are acquitted by our words or condemned by them. Proverbs 15:4 says a wholesome tongue is a tree of life: but perverseness therein is a breach in the spirit. I thank God for people who speak life into me, even when they point out areas of failure. We need to speak and receive words from the Tree of Life. This is so important that I included three chapters on the power of words in my book "Beat Me Up Spirits."[1]

Step five is choosing to become an over-comer. We are to be more than conquerors through Christ! Nothing can separate us from the love of God. We can do all things through Christ who strengthens us. Jesus calls us to listen, overcome, and eat from the Tree of Life.

📖 "He who has an ear, let him hear what the Spirit says to the churches. To him who overcomes I will give to eat from the tree of life, which is in the midst of the Paradise of God." Revelation 2:7.

Perhaps the biggest fear people face concerning the Tree of Life is that others might take advantage of their transparency and vulnerability, and use it to judge them rather than help them. Sadly, such is often true of some Christians and churches, but life-giving people are not like this.

Sixteen years ago I realized that I had spent most of my Christian life feeding from the tree of the knowledge of Good and Evil. I used to be more concerned about what people thought of me than what God thought. I dressed, talked and acted like people wanted me to dress, talk and act.

I remember from my teen years how my big sister swooned over the way a new male teacher swaggered when he walked. So I tried to add a swagger to my hips when I walked so I could be cool too. A good friend finally told me that I was walking like I had a corncob where it didn't belong and promised to help me overcome it by kicking me every time he caught me walking like that.

I went through similar stages as a young preacher. I remember trying to be like Bill Gothard, John Maxwell, Dr. Donald Howard, Jack Hyles and other men of God I looked up to. God helped me finally understand I needed to become who He created me to be rather than who He made others to be. God is the kind of friend who offers to teach us His perspective of wisdom and foolishness.

Earlier I shared how I judged one of my children for taking money from a school mate's wallet, and then how I judged myself as being unsuitable to pastor because I didn't manage my own household well. I not only judged myself from the tree of knowledge, but judged other ministers the same way until God gave me greater upstanding of "managing our own households well."

When I studied the Bible through the tree of knowledge, I was grieved by the qualifications given for church elders in First Timothy, Chapter Three. They seemed totally out of reach for me because my children were born in sin, just like their father. The verses which grieved me as a pastor and a father were verses 4-5.

📖 One who rules his own house well, having his children in submission with all reverence (for if a man does not know how to rule his own house, how will he take care of the church of God?) 1 Timothy 3:4-5.

The Lord helped me understand this passage from His point of view twenty years later. A dear pastor came to a Pastor's prayer group and was totally undone. He could barely talk through his tears. At first I wondered if his wife had left him for the church organist or something like that, but when he gained composure he asked us to pledge secrecy and admitted his teenage daughter was pregnant. He was convinced their only option was for his daughter to have an abortion so no one would ever know. This pastor feared his congregation and board might fire him if they found out the truth.

I tried to convince him having a child out of wedlock wasn't sin. The sin was having sex out of wedlock, not being pregnant. I offered to meet with his church and help walk the family and church through this circumstance in redemptive ways.

A minister rules his own house well if he deals with such issues from the tree of life, rather than the tree of the knowledge of good and evil. It is so much better to work through issues like this with transparency rather than secrecy. I wanted to help lead his church into grace flowing from the Tree of Life. I offered to share the first message I preached when I reentered ministry after my own fall. I wanted to preach from John 8 and the woman who was caught in the very act of adultery. They needed to learn mercy is more redemptive than judgment. In John 8, Jesus was the only perfect man in the crowd of accusers. Being perfect, he could have cast the first stone at the woman. Instead He said "neither do I condemn you, go and sin no more." As Jesus illustrated so well, true grace doesn't ignore sin but frees them to go and sin no more!

Unfortunately, for my pastor friend and his pregnant daughter, the fruit looked better from the tree of knowledge than from the tree of life. They kept their secret, took their daughter to a clinic, the baby's life was ended, and the family grieved alone. They hoped no one would ever find out, and perhaps it still remains hidden from people, but God knows.

The fruit looks good on the tree of knowledge. It tastes good. But it is it rotten. It is tempting to live in that tree, keeping our sins and needs secret. Chasing after titles, positions, and man's approval is as tempting as the fruit from the tree of knowledge was for Eve, but it will bring the same rotten fruit. I suggest the following prayer.

Breaking the Curse and Invoking the Blessing:

- I am redeemed from the Tree of the Knowledge of good and evil into the Tree of Life by the blood of the Lamb.
- Jesus, for far too long I've lived in and eaten fruit from the tree of the knowledge of good and evil.
- Today I confess and renounce the tree of knowledge and forgive those who have led me or judged me from that tree.
- You are the Tree of Life. I choose You this day. I choose to abide in You, remain in You, and live for You.
- I ask You to rebuke demons attached to me from the tree of knowledge. I resist those demons now, in Jesus' Name. (Expel)
- Please help me live in the Tree of Life and point out whenever I go back to the tree of knowledge and good and evil. Amen.
- I declare I am redeemed by the blood of the Lamb out of the hand of the enemy!

Endnotes Addendum:

[1] Dr. Douglas Carr, <u>Beat Me Up Spirits</u>, Create Space 2013.

Scriptures referred to but not quoted chapter and verse in this chapter include: John 1:14; 1 Corinthians 5:10; Genesis 1:2; John 14:6, 7:38, 15:1-8; James 4:8-10; Matthew 20:20-21; 1 Timothy 1:5; James 5:16; Romans 12:10; John 3:16-17; Ephesians 2:8-10; Acts 1:8; Luke 4:18; John 8:1-11, 10:10; Genesis 3:9; Luke 15:11-32; Matthew 11:28-30; Galatians 5:22-24; 1 John 1:9; Galatians 6:1-3; James 5:19-20; Deuteronomy 32:47; Proverbs 10:11, 15:4, John 6:63; Acts 5:20; James 3:13-17; Matthew 6:33, 12:37.

ABOUT THE AUTHOR

Dr. Douglas E. Carr was born again in 1972, and entered fulltime Christian ministry in 1973. He worked very hard at ministry and every church he pastored grew numerically, even though he lacked the spiritual depth to lead his people away from the tree of the knowledge of good and evil into the tree of life.

It took personal loss to bring Doug to where he cried out to know God personally. After fourteen years of ministry, he was broken and left "professional" ministry for five years. For Doug, it took personal failure to help him realize just how loving and merciful God really is.

Since 1992 Doug has been on the quest to know and share the love, acceptance, and forgiveness of God Almighty. He has come to know Holy Spirit personally and has great desire to lead people into freedom and victory.

Doug did his first deliverance in the mid-nineties. He soon sensed the call to lead others to freedom and began leading freedom appointments and Free Indeed Seminars.

In 1999, after a forty day fast, Doug was led to Wagner Leadership Institute where he earned his Masters and Doctorate with proficiencies in Deliverance and Intercession. While taking classes there he met Barbara Yoder and soon became part of her Breakthrough Apostolic Ministries Network.

Doug is truly blessed with His wife Pamela, and their five children and twenty-four grandchildren, and even a few great-grandchildren.

Doug and Pam pastor His House Foursquare Church in Sturgis, Michigan and continue to minister deep healing and deliverance, as well as lead Freed Indeed Seminars.

Other Titles by Dr. Douglas E. Carr:

Free Indeed ~ Deliverance Ministry.

Beat Me Up Spirits.

Free Indeed from Root Spirits.

Getting to the Dirty Rotten Inner Core.

Schematics: God's Blueprint versus Satan's Prog

God's Say So versus Man's Know So.

Let's Get Real.

Kingdom Thoughts 101.

Kingdom Thoughts 201.

All books are available through Amazon.co

For more information on Doug's ministry a
www.dougcarrfreedommministries.com

Endnotes Addendum:

[1] Dr. Douglas Carr, <u>Beat Me Up Spirits</u>, Create Space 2013.

Scriptures referred to but not quoted chapter and verse in this chapter include: John 1:14; 1 Corinthians 5:10; Genesis 1:2; John 14:6, 7:38, 15:1-8; James 4:8-10; Matthew 20:20-21; 1 Timothy 1:5; James 5:16; Romans 12:10; John 3:16-17; Ephesians 2:8-10; Acts 1:8; Luke 4:18; John 8:1-11, 10:10; Genesis 3:9; Luke 15:11-32; Matthew 11:28-30; Galatians 5:22-24; 1 John 1:9; Galatians 6:1-3; James 5:19-20; Deuteronomy 32:47; Proverbs 10:11, 15:4, John 6:63; Acts 5:20; James 3:13-17; Matthew 6:33, 12:37.

ABOUT THE AUTHOR

Dr. Douglas E. Carr was born again in 1972, and entered fulltime Christian ministry in 1973. He worked very hard at ministry and every church he pastored grew numerically, even though he lacked the spiritual depth to lead his people away from the tree of the knowledge of good and evil into the tree of life.

It took personal loss to bring Doug to where he cried out to know God personally. After fourteen years of ministry, he was broken and left "professional" ministry for five years. For Doug, it took personal failure to help him realize just how loving and merciful God really is.

Since 1992 Doug has been on the quest to know and share the love, acceptance, and forgiveness of God Almighty. He has come to know Holy Spirit personally and has great desire to lead people into freedom and victory.

Doug did his first deliverance in the mid-nineties. He soon sensed the call to lead others to freedom and began leading freedom appointments and Free Indeed Seminars.

In 1999, after a forty day fast, Doug was led to Wagner Leadership Institute where he earned his Masters and Doctorate with proficiencies in Deliverance and Intercession. While taking classes there he met Barbara Yoder and soon became part of her Breakthrough Apostolic Ministries Network.

Doug is truly blessed with His wife Pamela, and their five children and twenty-four grandchildren, and even a few great-grandchildren.

Doug and Pam pastor His House Foursquare Church in Sturgis, Michigan and continue to minister deep healing and deliverance, as well as lead Freed Indeed Seminars.

Other Titles by Dr. Douglas E. Carr:

Free Indeed ~ Deliverance Ministry.

Beat Me Up Spirits.

Free Indeed from Root Spirits.

Getting to the Dirty Rotten Inner Core.

Schematics: God's Blueprint versus Satan's Programming.

God's Say So versus Man's Know So.

Let's Get Real.

Kingdom Thoughts 101.

Kingdom Thoughts 201.

All books are available through Amazon.com

For more information on Doug's ministry and seminars visit: www.dougcarrfreedommministries.com

Made in the USA
Middletown, DE
20 June 2016